DEC 2014

1st EDITION

Perspectives on Modern World History

The McCarthy Era

1st EDITION

Perspectives on Modern World History

The McCarthy Era

Myra Immell

Book Editor

GREENHAVEN PRESS
A part of Gale, Cengage Learning

Detroit • New York • San Francisco • New Haven, Conn • Waterville, Maine • London

Christine Nasso, *Publisher*
Elizabeth Des Chenes, *Managing Editor*

© 2011 Greenhaven Press, a part of Gale, Cengage Learning.

Gale and Greenhaven Press are registered trademarks used herein under license.

For more information, contact:
Greenhaven Press
27500 Drake Rd.
Farmington Hills, MI 48331-3535
Or you can visit our Internet site at gale.cengage.com.

For product information and technology assistance, contact us at
Gale Customer Support, 1-800-877-4253.

For permission to use material from this text or product, submit all requests online at
www.cengage.com/permissions.

Further permissions questions can be e-mailed to permissionrequest@cengage.com.

Articles in Greenhaven Press anthologies are often edited for length to meet page requirements. In addition, original titles of these works are changed to clearly present the main thesis and to explicitly indicate the author's opinion. Every effort is made to ensure that Greenhaven Press accurately reflects the original intent of the authors. Every effort has been made to trace the owners of copyrighted material.

Cover image Custom Medical Stock Photo, Inc. Reproduced by permission.

LIBRARY OF CONGRESS CATALOGING-IN-PUBLICATION DATA

The McCarthy era / Myra Immell, book editor.
    p. cm. -- (Perspectives on modern world history)
  Includes bibliographical references and index.
ISBN 978-0-7377-5260-1 (hardcover)
1. Anti-communist movements--United States--History--20th century--Juvenile literature. 2. United States--History--1933–1945--Juvenile literature. 3. United States--History--1945–1953--Juvenile literature. 4. United States--Politics and government--1933–1953--Juvenile literature. 5. McCarthy, Joseph, 1908–1957--Biography--Juvenile literature. 6. Legislators--United States--Biography--Juvenile literature. 7. United States. Congress. Senate--Biography--Juvenile literature. I. Immell, Myra.
    E743.5.M368 2011
    973.921092--dc22
    [B]   2010043629

Printed in the United States of America
  2 3 4 5 6 7 15 14 13 12 11

CONTENTS

Ethel Rosenberg, the first American citizens to be executed for espionage, and discusses the unsuccessful attempts made to secure a reprieve for the couple.

CHAPTER 2   Controversies Surrounding the McCarthy Era

have to consider more carefully which statements and criticisms are truly worthy of being labeled "McCarthyism." He explains why some controversial statements and opinions are true.

CHAPTER **3**   Personal Narratives

FOREWORD

*"History cannot give us a program for the future,
but it can give us a fuller understanding of ourselves, and of our common humanity, so that we
can better face the future."*
                                    —Robert Penn Warren,
                                    American poet and novelist

The history of each nation is punctuated by momentous events that represent turning points for
that nation, with an impact felt far beyond its bor-
ders. These events—displaying the full range of human
capabilities, from violence, greed, and ignorance to hero-
ism, courage, and strength—are nearly always complicated and multifaceted. Any student of history faces the
challenge of grasping the many strands that constitute
such world-changing events as wars, social movements,
and environmental disasters. But understanding these
significant historic events can be enhanced by exposure
to a variety of perspectives, whether of people involved
intimately or of ones observing from a distance of miles
or years. Understanding can also be increased by learning about the controversies surrounding such events and
exploring hot-button issues from multiple angles. Finally,
true understanding of important historic events involves
knowledge of the events' human impact—of the ways
such events affected people in their everyday lives—all
over the world.

Perspectives on Modern World History examines
global historic events from the twentieth-century on-
ward by presenting analysis and observation from
numerous vantage points. Each volume offers high
school, early college level, and general interest readers

a thematically arranged anthology of previously published materials that address a major historical event, with an emphasis on international coverage. Each volume opens with background information on the event, then presents the controversies surrounding that event, and concludes with first-person narratives from people who lived through the event or were affected by it. By providing primary sources from the time of the event, as well as relevant commentary surrounding the event, this series can be used to inform debate, help develop critical thinking skills, increase global awareness, and enhance an understanding of international perspectives on history.

Material in each volume is selected from a diverse range of sources, including journals, magazines, newspapers, nonfiction books, personal narratives, speeches, congressional testimony, government documents, pamphlets, organization newsletters, and position papers. Articles taken from these sources are carefully edited and introduced to provide context and background. Each volume of Perspectives on Modern World History includes an array of views on events of global significance. Much of the material comes from international sources and from US sources that provide extensive international coverage.

Each volume in the Perspectives on Modern World History series also includes:

- A full-color **world map**, offering context and geographic perspective.

- An annotated **table of contents** that provides a brief summary of each essay in the volume.

- An **introduction** specific to the volume topic.

- For each viewpoint, a brief **introduction** that has notes about the author and source of the viewpoint, and that provides a summary of its main points.

- Full-color **charts**, **graphs**, **maps**, and other visual representations.
- Informational **sidebars** that explore the lives of key individuals, give background on historical events, or explain scientific or technical concepts.
- A **glossary** that defines key terms, as needed.
- A **chronology** of important dates preceding, during, and immediately following the event.
- A **bibliography** of additional books, periodicals, and Web sites for further research.
- A comprehensive **subject index** that offers access to people, places, and events cited in the text.

Perspectives on Modern World History is designed for a broad spectrum of readers who want to learn more about not only history but also current events, political science, government, international relations, and sociology—students doing research for class assignments or debates, teachers and faculty seeking to supplement course materials, and others wanting to improve their understanding of history. Each volume of Perspectives on Modern World History is designed to illuminate a complicated event, to spark debate, and to show the human perspective behind the world's most significant happenings of recent decades.

INTRODUCTION

The year was 1947. World War II was over, and the Cold War had begun. The Soviet Union, Great Britain, France, and the United States had worked together to help defeat the Nazis during the war. But by 1947 perceptions had changed a lot. No longer was the Soviet Union a trusted ally for the French, British, and Americans. Just the year before, at a college in Missouri, British prime minister Winston Churchill had delivered his "Iron Curtain" speech, warning of Soviet expansion, declaring that "from Stettin in the Baltic to Trieste in the Adriatic, an Iron Curtain has descended across the Continent" of Europe.

Americans especially became increasingly leery of Soviet moves to expand their power and feared they would spread communism worldwide. In the eyes of many, their previous ally was now a dangerous and unfriendly enemy—the "Red Menace." A growing number of Americans—policy makers and average citizens alike—agreed with the director of the Federal Bureau of Investigation (FBI), J. Edgar Hoover. When testifying before the House Committee on Un-American Activities (HUAC) in 1947, Hoover asserted that the Communist Party of the United States was:

> far better organized than were the Nazis in occupied countries prior to their capitulation. They are seeking to weaken America just as they did in their era of obstruction when they were aligned with the Nazis. Their goal is the overthrow of our government. . . . There is no doubt as to where a real communist's loyalty rests. Their allegiance is to Russia, not the United States.

In 1947 the first wave of HUAC hearings got underway. The committee had had its beginnings in 1938 as the Dies Committee of the US House of Representatives, formed to investigate disloyalty and subversive activities in the United States on the part of public employees, private citizens, and organizations. Early on, the committee had targeted Nazi sympathizers, but by 1947 its focus had changed from Nazis to Communists and the Communist threat. HUAC had a lot of power. Its members could subpoena witnesses and pressure them to name people they knew—or thought—were Communists or Communist sympathizers. It could press witnesses for other information as well—any kind of information the committee thought would help identify and bring down Communists and their sympathizers. When witnesses were not quick to respond to the committee's questions or, worse yet, refused to comply, the committee often branded them as "red" and cited them for contempt of Congress. Even though a great many Americans supported the committee, it often went too far. It was not unusual for committee members to make unclear and broad accusations against people and to assume someone was guilty of disloyalty to the United States because at some point in time he or she had been associated with an organization perceived as Communist or sympathetic to Communists.

Even though the committee investigated various industries, it became most famous for taking on Hollywood and the entertainment industry. During early hearings, HUAC asked witnesses not under suspicion to testify about any Communist activity in Hollywood they might know about or had heard rumors about. The committee subpoenaed nineteen witnesses it believed were Communists and called up eleven of them to testify. Ten of the eleven refused to answer the committee's questions and came to be known as the Hollywood Ten. Each was held in contempt and given a prison sentence. They were suspended without pay by their studios and blacklisted by the Hollywood community. Blacklisting did not end with the Hollywood Ten. It took on a life of its own and went on well into the 1950s. Anyone who refused to address the committee was blacklisted.

But HUAC was not the only group responsible for the growing number of artists blacklisted. Major Hollywood studios vowed "not [to] knowingly employ a communist" and to "take positive action" on "disloyal elements." Other groups with strong anti-Communist sentiments also contributed, blacklisting directors, writers, and others in film and in radio and television. Among these were the Federal Bureau of Investigation (FBI), the Senate Internal Security Subcommittee, private interest groups, and patriotic organizations, generally working in league with studio heads, network executives, sponsors, and advertising agencies.

Americans' fears were heightened further in 1948. That year HUAC subpoenaed Whittaker Chambers, an editor at *Time* magazine who had been a Communist in the past. Chambers testified that Alger Hiss, a former State Department official and president of the Carnegie Endowment for International Peace, had belonged to the same underground Communist cell he had. Hiss, he said, had supplied classified government documents to the Soviet Union in the 1930s when he worked for the State Department. Hiss appeared before HUAC and denied that he knew Chambers and proclaimed that he was not and never had been a member of the Communist Party. Shortly after, he filed a slander suit against Chambers. To back up his accusation, Chambers produced first a series of documents that came to be known as the Baltimore papers and then a microfilm he had kept hidden that contained photos of the documents he said he had been given by Hiss.

In 1949 Alger Hiss was tried for perjury. The jury, however, could not agree on a verdict and the judge ended up calling a mistrial. That same year, China became a Communist country and the Soviet Union, which now controlled more than half of Europe, exploded its first atomic bomb. Americans, already fearful of the Soviets and communism, saw the bomb as a threat to US national security. Many were convinced that the Soviets must have had outside help to create such a bomb, some of it from Communists within the United States.

By 1950 American distrust and fear of the Soviets, communism, and Communists was bordering on hysteria. Before the year was out, the nation was plunged into a tidal wave of anti-communism fervor. Early in the year Alger Hiss was indicted and brought to trial again for perjury. This time he was found guilty and sentenced to five years in prison. Hot on the heels of the Hiss trial came Senator Joseph McCarthy's "Enemies Within" speech in Wheeling, West Virginia, in which he charged that the US State Department was full of Communists and Communist sympathizers. For many, McCarthy's allegations rang true. After all, hadn't the Hiss case proved that Communists had been, and probably still were, high up in the US government? The timing of the speech could have not been better. It launched McCarthy's anti-Communist campaign, which was to envelop the country for the next four years.

A few months after McCarthy made his speech, two other events further fanned the flames. In May an American couple, Julius and Ethel Rosenberg, were arrested on charges of espionage and accused of giving atomic secrets to the Soviet Union. Then, in June, Communist North Korea invaded non-Communist South Korea, setting off the multinational Korean War. That same month a special report, "Red Channels, The Report of Communist Influence in Radio and Television," was distributed to network officials in New York City. The report listed more than 150 performers believed to be members of the Communist Party, Communist sympathizers, or associated with organizations considered to have Communist leanings. According to a study on blacklisting in the entertainment industry published in 1956 by the Fund for the Republic, "'Red Channels' marked the formal beginning of blacklisting in the radio-TV industry." The report, edited by former FBI agents, served as the basic document on blacklisting in radio and television during the McCarthy era. The fear of all things Communist, the intimidation, and the finger-pointing that had its start in the late 1940s was enveloping the nation and grew to become the hallmark of the McCarthy era.

World Map

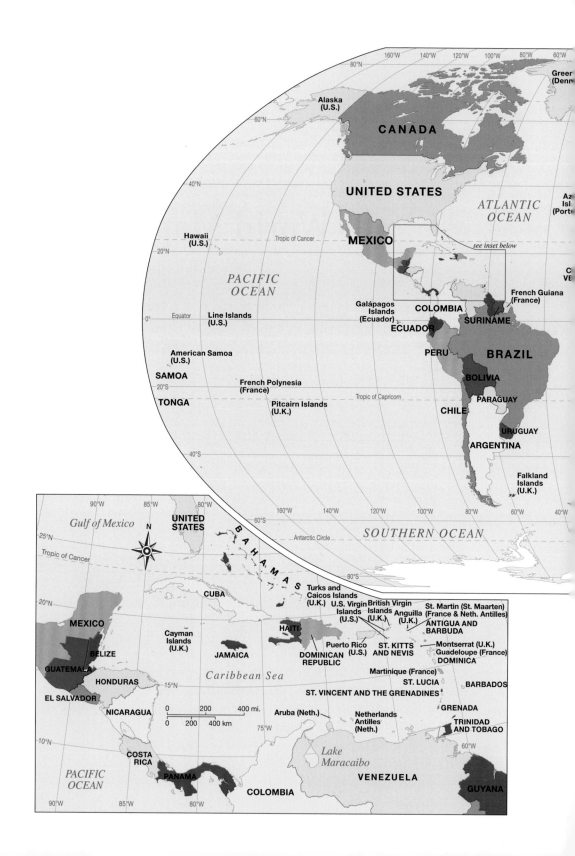

160°W 140°W 120°W 100°W 80°W 60°W

80°N

Green
(Denm

Alaska
(U.S.)

60°N

CANADA

40°N

UNITED STATES

ATLANTIC
OCEAN

Az
Isl
(Port

Hawaii
(U.S.)

Tropic of Cancer

20°N

MEXICO

see inset below

C
VE

PACIFIC
OCEAN

Galápagos
Islands
(Ecuador)

COLOMBIA

French Guiana
(France)

0°

Equator

Line Islands
(U.S.)

ECUADOR

SURINAME

American Samoa
(U.S.)

PERU

BRAZIL

SAMOA

French Polynesia
(France)

BOLIVIA

20°S

Tropic of Capricorn

PARAGUAY

TONGA

Pitcairn Islands
(U.K.)

CHILE

URUGUAY

ARGENTINA

40°S

Falkland
Islands
(U.K.)

160°W 140°W 120°W 100°W 80°W 60°W 40°W

60°S

SOUTHERN OCEAN

Antarctic Circle

80°S

90°W 85°W 80°W

Gulf of Mexico N

UNITED
STATES

B
A
H
A
M
A
S

25°N

Tropic of Cancer

CUBA

Turks and
Caicos Islands
(U.K.) U.S. Virgin British Virgin St. Martin (St. Maarten)
Islands Islands Anguilla (France & Neth. Antilles)
(U.S.) (U.K.) (U.K.) ANTIGUA AND
BARBUDA

20°N

MEXICO

Cayman
Islands
(U.K.)

HAITI

BELIZE

JAMAICA

Puerto Rico
(U.S.) ST. KITTS
AND NEVIS

Montserrat (U.K.)
Guadeloupe (France)
DOMINICA

GUATEMALA

DOMINICAN
REPUBLIC

Caribbean Sea

Martinique (France)
ST. LUCIA

BARBADOS

HONDURAS

15°N

ST. VINCENT AND THE GRENADINES

EL SALVADOR

GRENADA

0 200 400 mi.

NICARAGUA

Aruba (Neth.)

Netherlands
Antilles
(Neth.)

TRINIDAD
AND TOBAGO

0 200 400 km

75°W

60°W

10°N

COSTA
RICA

Lake
Maracaibo

PACIFIC
OCEAN

PANAMA

COLOMBIA

VENEZUELA

GUYANA

90°W 85°W 80°W

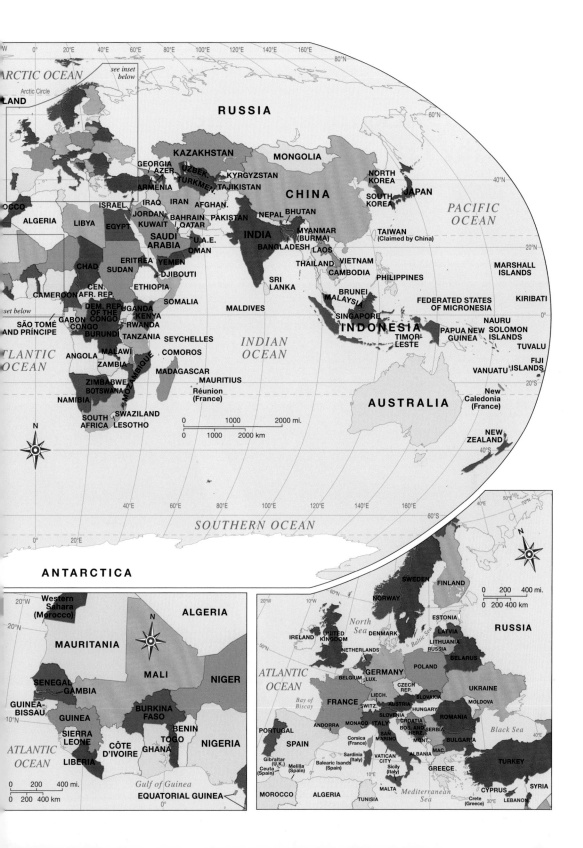

CHAPTER 1

Historical Background on the McCarthy Era

The McCarthy Era: An Overview

Joseph Patterson Hyder

In the following viewpoint from the multi-volume *Encyclopedia of Espionage, Intelligence, and Security*, Joseph Patterson Hyder provides an overview of the atmosphere and attitudes in the United States in the 1940s and 1950s. Americans' fear of a Communist takeover after World War II enabled Senator Joseph McCarthy to convince many of them that the US government was a hotbed of subversive elements and that any group or individual his committee identified as pro-Communist should be investigated, publicly vilified, and punished. Joseph Patterson Hyder is the managing partner for the Hyder Law Group in Jacksonville, Florida. He has written extensively on international treaties and political issues.

Photo on previous page: Wisconsin Senator Joseph McCarthy presided over Senate hearings in the 1950s during the so-called Red Scare—a time when many Americans were labeled Communists. (**Time & Life Pictures.**)

SOURCE. Joseph Patterson Hyder, "McCarthyism," *Encyclopedia of Espionage, Intelligence, and Security*. K. Lee Lerner and Brenda Wilmoth Lerner (eds), Vol. 2, Gale, a part of Cengage Learning, Inc. Reproduced by permission.

In the early 1950s, Joseph McCarthy, a U.S. Senator from Wisconsin, conducted highly publicized congressional hearings to uncover subversive elements within American culture, government, and military. For over three years, McCarthy used questionable means to uncover information about suspects. The McCarthy era represents the height of the post-war "Red scare" and demonstrates the degree to which paranoia about subversive communist activities had gripped America.

The Alien Registration Act Takes Hold

The wartime Alien Registration Act of 1940 laid the foundation for McCarthyism. This act required that all aliens over the age of 14 residing in the United States register with the American government. Each resident alien had to file a report detailing his or her political beliefs and work status. The act also made it illegal for anyone to plan to overthrow the government of the United States.

The Alien Registration Act had a twofold purpose. First, with American involvement in World War II likely, Congress hoped the act would help identify potential wartime saboteurs. The government wanted to avoid a repeat of the situation in World War I, when German-supported saboteurs and German sympathizers targeted American industry and shipping that aided the European war effort. By acquiring a detailed work history of aliens, the government sought to identify potential problems before they occurred. The second and primary objective of the Alien Registration Act was to identify elements of the American Communist Party or other socialist organizations.

Hollywood Suffers HUAC and the Blacklist

It was subsequently determined that the existing House Un-American Activities Committee (HUAC) would serve as the body that would seek out subversive elements. In

1947, HUAC began a campaign to rid Hollywood of all leftist elements. In a series of highly publicized congressional hearings, some individuals in the entertainment industry identified their peers as belonging to questionable leftist organizations, including the American Communist Party.

In an effort to avoid further embarrassing hearings and to regain public trust, Hollywood studios drew up a blacklist of individuals suspected of belonging to or having an interest in subversive organizations. These individuals found it difficult to work in Hollywood until they had cleared their names before HUAC. The blacklist included many well-known celebrities, including [actor and film director] Charlie Chaplin, [actor, writer, and folk music singer] Burl Ives, [composer and conductor] Leonard Bernstein, [classical composer] Aaron Copeland, and [playwright and essayist] Arthur Miller.

Senator Joseph McCarthy "sought to characterize the army as an organization riddled with subversive elements" during hearings in 1954. (Time & Life Pictures.)

> To the public, the threat of a complex communist plot to infiltrate American society and government seemed tangible.

The Hollywood blacklist and the HUAC hearings fed the atmosphere of suspicion that gripped American society. To the public, the threat of a complex communist plot to infiltrate American society and government seemed tangible. The high-profile HUAC hearings, combined with the well-publicized [Ethel and Julius] Rosenberg and Alger Hiss trials, served to reinforce this sentiment. In the fall of 1949, the government began a crackdown, arresting most of the leadership of the American Communist Party and charging them under the Alien Registration Act.

Joseph McCarthy Claims Communists Are in the Government

In February 1950, Joseph McCarthy became involved in the search for subversive elements within the government. McCarthy claimed to have a list containing the names of State Department employees belonging to the American Communist Party. McCarthy's list did not contain any arcane knowledge, having been compiled by the State Department several years earlier following an internal investigation. Additionally, most of the names were on the list for other questionable behaviors. Few members on the list had any current or previous ties to the Communist Party.

McCarthy took to the pulpit when he became chairman of the Government Committee on Operations of the Senate. Using his position, McCarthy began investigating possible communist infiltration of various government agencies. McCarthy worked closely with the Federal Bureau of Investigation [FBI] and his close friend [FBI director] J. Edgar Hoover. The FBI supplied McCarthy with the information that he needed to keep his committee hearings effective. Government employees found to have ties to the Communist Party or other left-wing groups were removed from office and forced to divulge the names of other individuals affiliated with leftist organizations.

McCarthy Broadens His Targets

McCarthy's committee also targeted the Overseas Library Program. The Government Committee on Operations of the Senate identified and banned over 30,000 books thought to have been written by communist sympathizers or to contain pro-communist themes. Many public libraries across the United States removed these books from their shelves.

McCarthy's operations further expanded into the realm of American politics. His committee conducted disinformation campaigns to thwart the reelection bids of politicians that opposed him. McCarthy even targeted the Truman administration, including President Harry S. Truman himself and cabinet member George Marshall, the renowned architect of the postwar Marshall Plan, for supporting the New Deal and for being perceived as soft on communism in Korea. McCarthy supported Dwight D. Eisenhower's presidential campaign in 1952, and in return, Eisenhower allowed McCarthy to continue his anti-communist hearings.

McCarthy Takes on the US Army

In October 1953, after nearly three years of targeting civilian agencies, McCarthy set his sights on identifying and removing subversive elements within the United States Army. Eisenhower, a former army general, decided to stop him. Vice-president Richard M. Nixon spoke out, asserting that McCarthy was motivated not by concern for his country but by a desire for personal aggrandizement. It was revealed that McCarthy had tried to prevent the army from drafting one of his staff members, G. David Schine. After failing in that attempt, Mc-

Anti-Communist Hysteria Sweeps the Country

McCarthy was, without a doubt, the most destructive anti-Communist of the time, but he was not the only one ruining careers and smearing reputations. Around the country, thousands of civil servants, schoolteachers, trade unionists, and scientists were driven from their jobs by witch hunts equal in viciousness to those mounted by the Wisconsin senator. Thousands of other citizens remained silent for fear that they, too, would be attacked. The hysteria had the quality of the ridiculous. Schools banned "Robin Hood" for its "Communist" themes. The Cincinnati Reds baseball team changed its name to the "Red Legs" for fear that anyone would receive the wrong idea. Mickey Spillane, author of the sensational Mike Hammer adventure stories, had his tough private eye go after agents of Communist subversion instead of the gangsters he had shot up in the early 1940s. And two years after he had broken baseball's color barrier and earned the respect of the nation, Jackie Robinson was called before the Un-American Activities Committee to testify about Communist influence in the black community.

SOURCE. *Peter Jennings and Todd Brewster, The Century. NY: Doubleday, 1998, p. 314.*

Carthy and his chief counsel, Roy Cohn, had petitioned [Secretary of the Army Robert] Stevens to grant special privileges to Schine. The Schine affair prompted McCarthy to target Secretary Stevens: when Stevens refused his request, McCarthy claimed that the army was holding Schine hostage in order to prevent his committee from uncovering communist elements within their ranks.

McCarthy determined that Congress should investigate the matter. He also sealed his fate by allowing television cameras to air the Army-McCarthy hearings. During the hearings, McCarthy and Cohn sought to characterize the army as an organization riddled with subversive elements. Throughout the hearings, McCarthy appeared rude to an attentive television audience. On the other hand, a personable attorney, Joseph Welch, represented the army. It was Welch who ultimately destroyed McCarthy's credibility with his retort to McCarthy, "Have you no sense of decency, sir, at long last? Have you left no sense of decency?" A bewildered McCarthy did not realize that the power that he once wielded had been crushed before a national television audience. In December 1954, Congress censured [issued a formal reprimand against] Joseph McCarthy by a vote of 67–22.

> "[McCarthy] sealed his fate by allowing television cameras to air the Army-McCarthy hearings."

President Truman Orders a Loyalty Check

Times (London) correspondent

The following viewpoint from the March 27, 1947, edition of the British newspaper the *Times* focuses on the executive order signed a week earlier by US president Harry S. Truman. The president maintains that the order is needed to keep disloyal and subversive individuals out of the US government and to protect loyal government employees from being unfairly accused of disloyalty. Under the order, more than two million executive branch employees would be checked for loyalty by the Federal Bureau of Investigation, as would anyone applying for a government position from then on. A list of all subversive organizations in the nation will be prepared and continually updated and a central master index kept of anyone whose loyalty has been investigated. As safeguards, loyalty boards will be formed to look into charges of disloyalty and employees charged with disloyalty will be able to state their case and have a right to counsel.

SOURCE. *Times* (London) Correspondent, "Purge of U.S. Civil Service," The *Times*, March 24, 1947. Reproduced by permission.

President [Harry S.] Truman has issued an executive order under which Government service is to be purged immediately of employees found to be disloyal or subversive. His sweeping order is directed not only at members but at "fellow-travellers" of any "totalitarian, Fascist, Communist, or subversive organization" and those believed to be in sympathetic association with organizations which seek to deny constitutional rights to others or to alter the form of Government in the United States by unconstitutional means.

The Washington, D.C., building that housed the Civil Service Commission, was also where President Truman's Loyalty Review Boards were established. (Time & Life Pictures/Getty Images.)

Loyalty Checks and Lists

The Federal Bureau of Investigation is to check the loyalty of some 2,000,000 employees of the executive branch of the Government, and the same organization will make a "loyalty check" of every future applicant for Government employment.

The Attorney-General by this order is directed to prepare and maintain in up-to-date condition a list of all subversive organizations in the United States while the Civil Service Commission will maintain a central master index of all persons whose loyalty has been investigated;

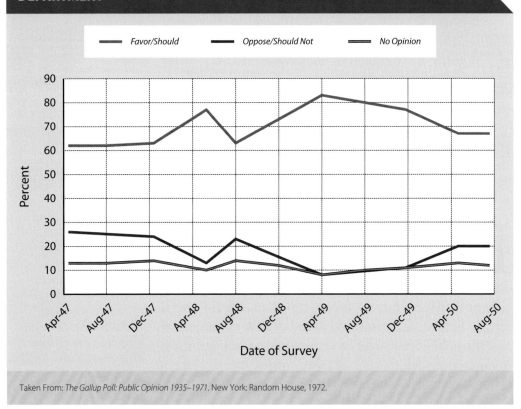

PUBLIC OPINION ON WHETHER THERE SHOULD BE A LAW REQUIRING COMMUNIST PARTY MEMBERS TO REGISTER WITH THE JUSTICE DEPARTMENT

Taken From: *The Gallup Poll: Public Opinion 1935–1971.* New York: Random House, 1972.

and material for this index is to be supplied by all agencies of the Government that have accumulated information of the loyalty of their employees.

The order applies only to officers and employees of executive departments and agencies of Government. Judicial and legislative branches are not involved, and the Army and Navy will continue their present security measures.

Safeguards Against Abuse

The President in his order has made safeguards against the abuse of it. Each department agency will have loyalty boards to investigate charges of disloyalty and employees so charged will be given a full opportunity to state their case, including the use of counsel.

Before this sweeping order can go into effect, however, it will be necessary to obtain from Congress appropriations amounting from 15,000,000 to 20,000,000 dollars to enlarge the staffs of the Civil Service Commission and the Bureau of Investigation, but beyond this no legislation is required, the President having acted under the so-called Hatch Act, sponsored by Senator Carl Hatch during the war to prevent "pernicious political activity."

> 'The presence within the Government service of any disloyal or subversive person constitutes a threat to our democratic processes.'

In his order the President pointed out that each employee of the Government is endowed with a measure of trusteeship over those democratic processes which are the heart and sinew of the United States, and said he took this drastic action because "the presence within the Government service of any disloyal or subversive person constitutes a threat to our democratic processes ... and maximum protection must be afforded the United States against the infiltration of disloyal persons in the ranks of its employees, and equal protection from unfounded accusations of disloyalty must be afforded loyal employees of the Government."

A Uniform Standard of Loyalty

His order has the effect of establishing one standard of loyalty for all detriments and agencies in contrast with a wide variety of standards which has prevailed in different sections of the Government. The grounds upon which reasonable doubt of disloyalty may be based include commission of sabotage or treason, advocacy of force to alter the form of government, deliberate disclosure of classified documents in circumstances which indicate disloyalty, and performance of official duties in such a way as to serve the interests of other Governments in preference to the interests of the United States. As far as membership of organizations is concerned the Attorney-General is to designate which are totalitarian, Fascist, Communist, or subversive.

The Execution of Julius and Ethel Rosenberg

Guardian

The following viewpoint from the June 20, 1953, British publication the *Guardian* focuses on the June 19 execution for espionage of Americans Julius and Ethel Rosenberg and the unsuccessful efforts to save them. The US Supreme Court set aside a stay of execution granted earlier in the week, and a few days later President Dwight Eisenhower rejected a final appeal for clemency. Rosenberg supporters gathered in London hoping for help from the British, but their last-minute appeals to Prime Minister Winston Churchill and Queen Elizabeth II to use their influence to secure a reprieve for the Rosenbergs proved futile.

Julius and Ethel Rosenberg were executed early this morning [June 19, 1953] at Sing Sing Prison for conspiring to pass atomic secrets to Russia in World War II.

SOURCE. "Execution of the Rosenbergs: 'Enemies of Democracy'," The *Guardian*, June 20, 1953. Reproduced by permission.

Only a few minutes before, [US] President [Dwight D.] Eisenhower had rejected a last desperate plea written in her cell by Ethel Rosenberg. Mr. Emanuel Bloch, the couple's lawyer, personally took the note to the White House, where guards turned him away.

Neither of the two said anything before they died. The news of their execution was announced at 1:45 A.M. (British time).

Execution Day

New York, June 19

Julius and Ethel Rosenberg were executed in the electric chair at Sing Sing Prison tonight. Neither husband nor wife spoke before they died.

Julius Rosenberg, aged 35, was the first to die. They were executed just before the setting sun heralded the Jewish Sabbath. Prison officials had advanced the execution time to spare religious feelings.

Mrs. Rosenberg turned just before she was placed in the electric chair, drew Mrs Evans, the prison matron, towards her, and they kissed. The matron was visibly affected. She quickly turned and left the chamber. In the corridor outside, Rabbi Irving Koslowe could be heard intoning the 23rd Psalm.

The couple were the first civilians in American history to be executed for espionage. They were sentenced to death on April 5, 1951, for passing on atomic secrets to Russia during the Second World War.

President Eisenhower's Decision Not to Intervene

The last hope of reprieve for the Rosenbergs vanished early this afternoon when President Eisenhower rejected a final appeal for clemency shortly after the Supreme Court had set aside the stay of execution granted by Justice [William O.] Douglas, one of its own members, on

Photo on previous page: Julius (right) and Ethel Rosenberg were convicted of espionage and executed on June 19, 1953. (**Associated Press.**)

Monday. The President's decision was announced in the following statement from the White House:

Since the original review of proceedings in the Rosenberg case by the Supreme Court of the United States, the courts have considered numerous further proceedings challenging the Rosenbergs' conviction and the sentencing involved. Within the last two days, the Supreme Court convened in a special session and reviewed a further point which one of the justices felt the Rosenbergs should have an opportunity to present. This morning the Supreme Court ruled that there was no substance to this point.

> 'Throughout the innumerable complications and technicalities of this case no Judge has ever expressed any doubt that [the Rosenbergs] committed most serious acts of espionage.'

I am convinced that the only conclusion to be drawn from the history of this case is that the Rosenbergs have received the benefits of every safeguard which American justice can provide. There is no question in my mind that their original trial and the long series of appeals constitute the fullest measure of justice and due process of law. Throughout the innumerable complications and technicalities of this case no Judge has ever expressed any doubt that they committed most serious acts of espionage.

Accordingly, only most extraordinary circumstances would warrant Executive intervention in the case. I am not unmindful of the fact that this case has aroused grave concern both here and abroad in the minds of serious people aside from the considerations of law. In this connection I can only say that, by immeasurably increasing the chances of atomic war, the Rosenbergs may have condemned to death tens of millions of innocent people all over the world. The execution of two human beings is a grave matter. But even graver is the thought of millions of dead, whose death may be directly attributable to what these spies have done.

When democracy's enemies have been judged guilty of a crime as horrible as that of which the Rosenbergs were convicted: when the legal processes of democracy have been marshalled to their maximum strength to protect the lives of convicted spies: when in their most solemn judgement the tribunals of the United States has adjudged them guilty and the sentence just. I will not intervene in this matter.

Failed Last-Minute Pleas

President Eisenhower's decision came about half an hour after Mr. Emanuel Bloch, the Rosenberg's chief lawyer, had addressed an impassioned appeal to him, declaring that the world would be shocked if the execution was carried out with, he said, so much doubt in the case. He demanded that the President should find himself time "to consider this serious matter" and argued that rejection of the clemency appeal would jeopardise the United State's relation with its allies. "Tens of millions throughout the world condemn the death sentence," he added. "For the sake of American tradition, prestige and influence I urge redress for the Rosenbergs."

Less than four hours before the execution, Mr Bloch announced the failure of yet another attempt to gain a stay—a separate plea to Justice [Harold H.] Burton, one of nine members of the Supreme Court—to Reuters and British United Press.

The British Prime Minister's Response

A deputation from a "Save the Rosenbergs" protest meeting held at Marble Arch, London last night, called at No. 10 Downing Street [London residence of the British prime minister] where it was told the Prime Minister [Winston Churchill] was at Chartwell [Churchill's personal residence]. Members of the deputation, which was led by the Rev. Stanley Evans, then motored to Chartwell.

When they arrived in the lane outside Sir Winston's home, Mr. Evans and [Marxist scientist] Professor [J.D.] Bernal found about twenty supporters of the National Rosenberg Defence Committee. They had scribbled a note addressed "Dear P.M.," and asking the Prime Minister to appeal direct "to President Eisenhower over the Transatlantic telephone immediately." In reply they received a typewritten note saying: "It is not within my duty or my power to intervene in this matter. (Signed) Winston Churchill."

> 'It is not within my duty or my power to intervene in this matter. (Signed) Winston Churchill.'

This reply was handed to the deputation at midnight, and the gates of Chartwell were closed for the night.

At the End of the Wait

In London, fifty demonstrators who had earlier stated they intended to keep an all-night vigil at No. 10 Downing Street found police had cordoned off both entrances by the time they arrived at 12.50 A.M.

At one o'clock this morning in Manchester a crowd of two hundred stood quietly outside the offices of the "Manchester Guardian" waiting for news of the Rosenberg executions.

The crowd stood in silence until the executions were announced at 1:45 A.M. The news was received in silence, and members of the crowd, most of them men, maintained a two minutes' silence for the Rosenbergs. Afterwards they moved off to the steps of the Royal Exchange in Cross Street where the meeting pledged itself to continue the fight to clear the name of the Rosenbergs and "to pin the blame where it rightly belongs."

A telegram sent earlier to the Queen had asked her to use her influence towards securing a reprieve.

A Look into One Day of McCarthy-Army Hearings

Washington Post

The following article from the April 24, 1954, edition of the *Washington Post* offers insights into the mood and tone of one session of the highly publicized, televised McCarthy-Army hearings, which got underway that March and ended three months later. Using a series of anecdotes picked up from different news service accounts, the viewpoint describes the actions, interactions, and reactions of some of the session participants and members of the audience. It highlights some of the lighter moments of the day, such as a photographer snapping a picture of a secret document and everyone laughing with Senator McCarthy at his response to the Senate Investigation Committee chairman's statement that his "time [had] expired."

SOURCE. "Cameraman 'Steals' Secrets Before Eyes of Probers," *Washington Post,* April 24, 1954. Reproduced by permission.

*H*ere are some highlights of the McCarthy-Army hearing yesterday, gleaned from news service accounts of the session:

A Secret Caught on Film

The biggest laugh yet at the tense McCarthy-Army hearings came when a witness held up a still-secret document and a photographer took a picture of it.

John J. Lucas, Jr., appointment clerk to Secretary of the Army [Robert T.] Stevens, was in the witness chair. Senator [Henry M.] Jackson (D-Wash.) asked him how many words there were in a transcription of a monitored telephone call between Stevens and Senator [Joseph R.] McCarthy.

Lucas referred first to his shorthand notes, said it was hard to estimate from that, and asked if he could refer to the typed version of his notes. This was permitted.

Then Lucas lifted up the typed document—and an alert photographer snapped a picture of it. Sen. McCarthy (R-Wis.) protested that this was no way to treat a document which hadn't even been admitted for evidence.

> *The biggest laugh yet at the tense McCarthy-Army hearings came when a witness held up a still-secret document and a photographer took a picture of it.*

The photographer, Hank Walker of *Life* magazine, settled the issue by destroying the film so everyone could see.

Applause, Crowd Control, and Not Enough Microphones

Senator McCarthy didn't get the hand he received Thursday when he walked into the crowded Senate caucus room. Just before the Wisconsin Senator entered, Karl E. Mundt (R-S. Dak.), acting chairman of the Senate Investigations Subcommittee, asked spectators to refrain from

applause. All followed instructions including a few who wore red-white-and-blue lapel buttons reading, "I'm for McCarthy."

Capitol police were using theater-usher tactics to regulate the flow of spectators. When any seats fell vacant, a guard inside would signal the man on the door, holding up an appropriate number of fingers. The crowd outside the Senate caucus room was smaller than Thursday's, but there was always a waiting line, and standees were banked solidly along the walls.

Senate aide Roy Cohn, Senator Joseph McCarthy, and aide Francis Carr (left to right) share a laugh in a lighter moment during the hearings. (Associated Press.)

The Cost of Live Television Coverage

Convened on 22 April 1954, the [Army-McCarthy] hearings . . . would preempt 35 days of regular telecasts and consume around 187 hours of airtime. At the outset, the Columbia Broadcasting System (CBS) declined to offer live coverage, fearing the loss of revenue from its daytime shows. . . . The National Broadcasting Company (NBC) telecast the sessions live the first two days before withdrawing because of scant viewer interest and substantial losses in advertising money (the [Senate] subcommittee did not permit commercial sponsorship of broadcasts of the first two weeks of the hearings). NBC, which provided 45-minute summaries of the hearings daily throughout the investigation, as did CBS, lost $125,000 over those two days of live coverage . . . and stood to lose $300,750 weekly if it continued with expensive live telecasts of the slow-paced hearings. The ten-day cost of the coverage alone was projected at more than nine million dollars for all networks.

The American Broadcasting Company (ABC) and the Du Mont network offered live coverage throughout the hearings, although some stations dropped the telecasts. Virtually without daytime programming, ABC, which supplied programs to just fifty to seventy-nine stations, and Du Mont, which numbered only ten stations, lost no advertising revenue and could afford public affairs telecasts. Furthermore, because the American Telephone & Telegraph Company, whose cables linked the two networks' stations, charged ABC and Du Mont for a whole day and evening of transmission, even if the networks were not providing programs, the networks had no reason not to televise the hearings.

SOURCE. *Michael Gauger, "Flickering Images: Live Television Coverage and Viewership of the Army-McCarthy Hearings," The Historian, Winter 2005, pp. 681–682.*

Microphones were all over the place but Army Counsel Joseph N. Welch didn't have one. He asked Mundt to use his "enormous power" to correct the deficiency. Mundt's enormous power wasn't enough. The electricians had everything hooked up in such a way there wasn't room for another mike.

McCarthy: Outtalked and Restricted

John J. Lucas, Jr., Stevens' appointments secretary, observed that transcripts of Congressional hearings always read perfectly. "That is why I know they are not very exact," he testified.

Subcommittee Counsel Ray H. Jenkins demonstrated that a lawyer can out-talk a Senator on the Senator's home grounds. At one point in the hearing, Jenkins and Senator McCarthy got into a noisy contest for the public address system after both began talking at the same time.

> Subcommittee Counsel Ray H. Jenkins demonstrated that a lawyer can out-talk a Senator on the Senator's home grounds.

Jenkins' Tennessee drawl finally won control of the amplifier. He told McCarthy the Senator could talk later but meantime his remarks were not in order.

A moment later Chairman Mundt let McCarthy state his argument. After hearing it, Jenkins conceded that McCarthy was right.

When McCarthy reached the end of one of his 10-minute interrogation periods, Mundt told him his "time has expired." McCarthy feigned concern, "You mean time for questioning, I assume," he said. Both Senators joined in the general laughter.

Additional Hearing Highlights

Mundt ran into a problem when he ordered one exchange stricken from the record. How, asked Senator Henry M. Jackson (D-Wash.), could Mundt strike something that already had been heard across the Nation via radio and television. The Chairman thought this one over for a moment and said: "Leave it in the record."

One woman who couldn't get a seat stood on a table at the rear of the hearing room and watched the proceedings through opera glasses. Presumably she saw almost as much as she could have at home on television.

Assistant Deputy Attorney General Robert W. Minor was in the audience but he cautioned not to misunderstand his presence. "It's my day off," he explained.

McCarthy Remains Popular with Many Voters

Al L. Otten, David O. Ives, and William A. Otark

In the following article from the October 15, 1954, edition of the *Wall Street Journal,* three writers report that even though Senator Joseph McCarthy's popularity has fallen, especially among members of his own political party, he remains very popular with many American voters. They state that, while many Republicans and Democrats think he has been doing a good job that needed to be done—ferreting out and ridding the government of Communists—some do not approve of his methods. One clear sign of McCarthy's continuing widespread popularity, they report, is that most Democratic and Republican candidates will not attack him for fear of losing votes. McCarthy, the authors conclude, remains an important political force whose demise has been greatly exaggerated. At the time this viewpoint was written, Al L. Otten, David O. Ives, and William A. Otark were reporters for the *Wall Street Journal.*

SOURCE. Al L. Otten, David O. Ives, and William A. Otark, "Political Demise? While the Pundits Write Off McCarthy, Many Voters Like Him as Much as Ever," *Wall Street Journal,* October 15, 1954. Reproduced by permission.

A number of writers and politicians may have buried Wisconsin's controversial Senator Joseph R. McCarthy—but a great many voters haven't.

The Senator's popularity has fallen sharply in recent months, to be sure. The dip is particularly noticeable among members of his own party. But the surprising fact confirmed by talks with hundreds of voters around the country is not how much Mr. McCarthy's rating has dipped, but how high it still is with sizable blocs of both Democrats and Republicans.

> 'As soon as a guy like McCarthy tries to do a job that needs to be done, they all gang up on him and try to stop him.'

Said the executive of a Chicago sales promotion firm just after the Watkins Committee recommended censure of Senator McCarthy for contempt of the Senate: "I sent Joe a telegram telling him I was 100% for him. You can't fight fire with talcum powder." There is every indication that the Senate group's findings are having little effect on what the public thinks of Joe. The public had already pretty well made up its mind.

No Lack of Strong Opinions

That's one of the remarkable things about Mr. McCarthy. Nearly everybody has opinions about him, usually very strong ones. Ask the man on the street about his views on foreign aid, farm policy or German rearmament and the answer is frequently, "I don't know," in one version or another. Ask about Joe McCarthy, and nearly every time you'll evoke denunciation or praise.

"Maybe his methods aren't just right," one often hears, "but you have to be tough with Communists." "Those politicians," snaps a Lewiston, Idaho, cab-driver. "As soon as a guy like McCarthy tries to do a job that needs to be done, they all gang up on him and try to stop him."

In Newark, N.J., a scaffold-rigger said: "I think he's doing a fine job. He hasn't done a thing wrong. In the end, the country will be very thankful." An Evansville, Ind., housewife, whose husband works for Chrysler, feels "we need more men like McCarthy. Those people who plead the Fifth Amendment are all guilty in my eyes."

Strong Pro-McCarthy Attitudes Among Democrats

The pro-McCarthy sentiment is found almost as much among Democrats in some areas as among Republicans. In St. Paul, the wife of a musician is going to vote Republican for the first time in her life. "I've always been a Democrat," she says, "but I think McCarthy is doing a fine job and I'm frightened by the way the Democrats handled him in those Army hearings. I'm for whoever he's for, and he's a Republican so I'm voting Republican."

A sales-clerk in a Trenton, N.J., department store believes "they should let him go ahead and get the Communists out. I've always been a Democrat, but that's one thing I think the Democrats are doing wrong."

Frequently, the McCarthy admirers are for him because "he puts on a good fight." Democrat Joseph Andrews, a newspaper printer in Springfield, Ill., approves of Mr. McCarthy because "he's a scrapper. Some of these Communists in Government and industry are hard to root out." And, in the opinion of a San Francisco janitor, "he may not fight according to the rules, but he's got more guts than the rest of those guys."

A Two-Edged Sword: Political Attacks on McCarthy

The fact that Republican party officials and G.O.P. [Grand Old Party] candidates in the various states were slow this fall in asking Senator McCarthy to speak for them has been widely cited as an instance of his fall in popularity. This is correct. But it's equally true—and much less widely cited—that the failure of most Democratic or Republican candidates to attack the Senator is a sure sign of very widespread continued McCarthy popularity. Except in New Jersey and one of two other areas, both Republican and Democratic candidates have been extremely careful to avoid attacking him.

In Massachusetts, where former Representative Foster Furcolo is challenging Republican Senator Leverett Saltonstall, "it's almost as though [the candidates] have a gentleman's agreement not to talk about McCarthy," says one Bay State politician. And the same is true of most other states. Both sides are realizing that "the McCarthy issue" is a two-edged one—that an attack on the Senator can lose votes as well as gain them. This has been especially a problem for many Democratic candidates since the McCarthy followers have been numerous among the Irish, Poles and other traditionally-Democratic voting blocs.

Origins of a Slump: Methods, Not Intent

Where the Senator's popularity has slumped, the usual reason is that "I approve of his aims but I don't like his methods." The drop in popularity occurred not so much during the recent censure hearings as during earlier investigations that McCarthy presided over and during the McCarthy-Army row. Many citizens felt that "he browbeat witnesses too much." They didn't like his use of supposedly secret papers or his general attitude towards the committee hearing the Army-McCarthy dispute. He lost many G.O.P. supporters who felt he was all right when he attacked Democrats but went too far when he attacked Republicans, too.

Says a San Francisco attorney who is a Republican party official: "He has become a menace to the country

> 'It's good to get the Communists out of Government, but he's using Communist methods.'

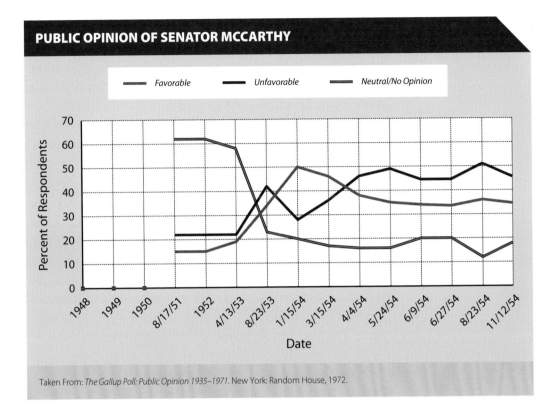

PUBLIC OPINION OF SENATOR MCCARTHY

Legend: Favorable — Unfavorable — Neutral/No Opinion

Y-axis: Percent of Respondents (0–70)

X-axis: Date (1948, 1949, 1950, 8/17/51, 1952, 4/13/53, 8/23/53, 1/15/54, 3/15/54, 4/4/54, 5/24/54, 6/9/54, 6/27/54, 8/23/54, 11/12/54)

Taken From: *The Gallup Poll: Public Opinion 1935–1971*. New York: Random House, 1972.

and a very serious liability to the Republican party." A Portland, Ore., newspaperman, also a registered Republican, swung against McCarthy during the Army hearings. "It's O.K. for a politician to say nasty things about people they don't like," he says. "They all do it. But when they start trying to run the whole Government, they have to be stopped."

Carrel Cocagne, who drives a gas truck for a farm-supply firm in Owaneco, Ill., feels that "It's good to get the Communists out of Government, but he's using Communist methods. What he's doing is destroying the people's faith in their Government." Frequently, the recently converted opponents of McCarthy use the phrase "he has no decency" in describing their reasons for switching. "Before the Army hearings, I didn't particularly like Joe's methods, but I thought he was doing a good job and that I had to overlook his methods," says a retired Boston businessman. "But after watching him on TV, I'm convinced that he simply is not a moral kind of man. I can never be for him again."

Of course, some voters have always been against McCarthy—especially Democratic voters. A welder at the Bucyrus-Erie plant in Evansville says he "always felt that if there are Communists in Government, Congress should pass a law and then leave it up to the F.B.I. and other law enforcement agencies. Members of Congress shouldn't run around doing all this investigating." George Thompson, a San Francisco salesman, declares he "knew McCarthy was dangerous when he was attacking [Secretary of State Dean] Acheson and General [George] Marshall, and he's gotten worse and worse since then. I'm glad the Republicans are beginning to see it."

A Hands On or Off Dilemma

Some, like a Trenton, N.J., letter-carrier, feel that the President should have been tougher with Mr. McCarthy. "I think Eisenhower should have spoken out and held McCarthy within proper bounds," he declares. But in Evanston, Ill., a pharmaceutical house salesman who voted for Ike, is mad because the President "should have kept his hands off the McCarthy fight. Some of those men who could have helped McCarthy were definitely gagged."

However much Joe's popularity has slipped, talks with citizens around the country make it plain that he must still be reckoned with as an important force because he's still surprisingly popular. The reports of McCarthy's political death so far seem to have been greatly exaggerated.

CHAPTER 2

Controversies Surrounding the McCarthy Era

The Loyalty Program Will Protect Individuals' Freedoms

Harry S. Truman

In the following viewpoint, a statement made November 14, 1947, on the Federal Employee Loyalty Program, Harry S. Truman acknowledges the need to remove disloyal employees from government positions. He maintains that most government employees are loyal and that those suspected of disloyalty must be treated fairly because the government must guarantee that the civil rights of all employees are protected at all times. Truman contends that the new loyalty program contains safeguards to protect the rights of those accused of disloyalty, including the serving of written notice of the charges, the opportunity to respond to the charges, hearings conducted by loyalty boards, right to counsel, and right of appeal to a department head and the Loyalty Review Board within the Civil Service Commission. Harry S. Truman was the thirty-third president of the United States.

Photo on previous page: A 1935 poster glorifies Joseph Stalin (left) and Soviet military might, which many Americans regarded as a threat. (Getty Images.)

SOURCE. Harry S. Truman, "Statement by the President on the Government's Employee Loyalty Program," *Public Papers of the President,* Harry S. Truman Library and Museum, November 14, 1947.

I deeply appreciate the willingness of the members of the Loyalty Review Board, established within the Civil Service Commission, to give of their service to that Board. Their acceptance involves real personal sacrifice. At the same time, they will have the satisfaction of knowing that they are contributing to the solution of one of the most difficult problems confronting our Government today.

Employees Need Not Fear the Loyalty Program

I believe I speak for all the people of the United States when I say that disloyal and subversive elements must be removed from the employ of the Government. We must not, however, permit employees of the Federal Government to be labeled as disloyal or potentially disloyal to their Government when no valid basis exists for arriving at such a conclusion. The overwhelming majority of Federal employees are loyal citizens who are giving conscientiously of their energy and skills to the United States. I do not want them to fear they are the objects of any "witch hunt." They are not being spied upon; they are not being restricted in their activities. They have nothing to fear from the loyalty program, since every effort has been made to guarantee full protection to those who are suspected of disloyalty. Rumor, gossip, or suspicion will not be sufficient to lead to the dismissal of an employee for disloyalty.

> Rumor, gossip, or suspicion will not be sufficient to lead to the dismissal of an employee for disloyalty.

Any person suspected of disloyalty must be served with a written notice of the charges against him in sufficient detail to enable him to prepare his defense. In some unusual situations security considerations may not allow full disclosure.

Loyalty Boards Will Ensure Fair Hearings

It would have been possible for the Government to remove disloyal persons merely by serving them with the charges against them and giving them an opportunity to answer those charges. I realize fully, however, the stigma attached to a removal for disloyalty. Accordingly, I have ordered the agencies of the Government, except where a few agencies find it necessary to exercise extraordinary powers granted to them by the Congress, to give hearings to persons who are charged with disloyalty.

Loyalty boards are being set up in each agency for this purpose. They are definitely not "kangaroo" courts. The personnel of these boards is being carefully selected by the head of each agency to make sure that they are judicious in temperament and fair-minded. Hearings before the boards will be conducted so as to establish all pertinent facts and to accord the suspected employee every possible opportunity to present his defense. The employee is to be given the right to be accompanied by counsel or a representative of his own choosing.

Avenues of Appeal

After the hearing has been completed the loyalty board in each department can recommend the retention or the dismissal of an employee. But the matter does not rest there. The employee may appeal the findings of the loyalty board to the head of the department, who can either approve or disapprove the board's recommendations.

If the head of the department orders the dismissal of the employee, he has still another avenue of appeal: namely, to the Loyalty Review Board within the Civil Service Commission. This Board is composed of outstanding citizens of the United States. These citizens have no ax to grind. They will not be concerned with personalities. Their judgment will be as detached as is humanly possible.

Photo on following page: President Truman issued an executive order in 1947 to root out government employees with sympathies toward "subversive organizations," including Communist ones. (Associated Press.)

Strictly a Political Problem

[Special counsel to the president] Clark Clifford would say sadly years later that the whole program had been "a response to the temper of the times," and that he did not see how Truman could have done otherwise.

But in an interview with the journalist Carl Bernstein, Clifford was considerably more blunt:

It was a political problem. [Clifford told Bernstein] Truman was going to run in '48, and that was it. . . .

My own feeling was there was not a serious problem. I felt the whole thing was being manufactured. We never had a serious discussion about a real loyalty problem. . . . the President didn't attach fundamental importance to the so-called Communist scare. He thought it was a lot of baloney. But political pressures were such that he had to recognize it. . . .

There was no substantive problem. . . . We did not believe there was a real problem. A problem was being manufactured. . . .

And politically the effect of Executive Order No. 9835 [the loyalty program] was indeed pronounced, for the moment at least, as *Time*'s Capitol Hill correspondent, Frank McNaughton, described in a confidential report to his editors:

The Republicans are now taking Truman seriously. . . . [His] order to root out subversives from government employment hit a solid note with Congress, and further pulled the rug from under his political detractors. The charge of "Communists in government" and nothing being done about it, a favorite theme of the reactionaries, simply will not stick any longer. . . . The Republicans are beginning to realize Truman is no pushover.

SOURCE. *David McCullough, Truman. NY: Simon & Schuster, 1992, pp. 552–553.*

Roles of Two Federal Government Agencies and the Loyalty Review Board

I expect the Civil Service Commission to function in a very real sense as a staff agency of the President for the purpose of doing everything it can to help him see to it that all aspects of this program are carried forward in an expeditious and satisfactory manner.

I am looking to the Federal Bureau of Investigation for the conduct of all loyalty investigations which may be necessary in connection with the operation of the program.

I am looking to the Loyalty Review Board to develop standards for the conduct of hearings and the consideration of cases within the various departments and agencies. With the cooperation of the staff of the Civil Service Commission, the Board should make sure that there is complete understanding of and adherence to these standards in all the departments and agencies.

The Importance of Standards

The question of standards is of deep concern to me. Under the Executive Order inaugurating this program, provision has been made, for example, for furnishing to the Loyalty Review Board by the Attorney General the name of each foreign or domestic organization, association, movement, group, or combination of persons which he, after appropriate investigation and determination, has designated as totalitarian, fascist, communist, or subversive. The Executive order in turn provides that the Loyalty Review Board shall disseminate such information to all departments and agencies.

This provision of the order has been interpreted by some to mean that any person who at any time happened to belong to one of these organizations would automatically be dismissed from the employ of the Federal Government.

A Flawed Interpretation

This interpretation completely overlooks the fact that, under the provisions of the Executive order, "the standard for the refusal of employment or the removal from employment in an executive department or agency on grounds relating to loyalty shall be that, on all the evidence, reasonable grounds exist for belief that the person involved is disloyal to the government of the United States."

> [The Government] must guarantee that the civil rights of all employees of the Government shall be protected properly and adequately.

Membership in an organization is simply one piece of evidence which may or may not be helpful in arriving at a conclusion as to the action which is to be taken in a particular case.

The Government has a great stake in these loyalty proceedings. The Government, as the largest employer in the United States, must be the model of a fair employer. It must guarantee that the civil rights of all employees of the Government shall be protected properly and adequately. It is in this spirit that the loyalty program will be enforced.

The Loyalty Program Does Not Safeguard Individuals' Freedoms

Chester E. Holifield

In the following viewpoint—a speech made June 27, 1947, on President Harry S. Truman's loyalty program—Chester E. Holifield warns of the dangers inherent in the loyalty program. He expresses concern that the methods proposed to determine whether an individual is loyal or disloyal lead to character assassination, a technique used successfully against opponents in the past and still in use in the present. Furthermore, the provisions to defend against an accuser, he contends, are too broad and give the attorney general power over civil liberties that until that point had belonged to the courts. He warns that suppressing civil liberties and being intemperate and intolerant will open the door to communism and fascism and destroy American democracy instead of protecting it. When this speech was given, Chester E. Holifield was a congressman from California in the US House of Representatives.

SOURCE. Chester E. Holifield, "Speech on Truman's Loyalty Program," June 27, 1947.

I wish to express today my deep concern over a new and dangerous tendency in American life, which I think threatens the very existence of the United States as a free nation.

A Threat to American Democracy

I do not refer to any growth of communism or fascism as such, but I do refer to the conduct of those who are most vocal in their efforts to—they say—"defend us against communism and fascism."

These people, while castigating individuals and organizations as being Communist or Fascist, deny these same individuals or organizations the right of a fair trial, the right of self-defense, the right of equal opportunity, to publicize their defense, against their accusers. . . .

We all know that the very root of our democracy is in the freedom and opportunity of each American to think for himself, to speak his thoughts to his neighbor, and that his ability to do so depends, most importantly of all, upon the freedom of his neighbors to speak their minds, upon any subject, without fear of reprisal or oppression.

If the expression of all points of view is in any respect curtailed, or citizens are to that extent deprived of the opportunity to reach their own conclusions, they are deprived of the founding fathers' principle of free speech, and free assembly, and therefore the play and interplay of free ideas among free men. . . .

A Dangerous But Successful Technique: Character Assassination

Let us then review some of the dangerous practices of today. During the 1946 campaign, the red-smearing technique of [Nazi Germany leader Adolf] Hitler was used, and used successfully, to retire many progressive men from public life. Men whose patriotism was unquestioned, men who stood for the best principles of American democracy.

But they found themselves helpless against the insidious technique of character assassination. . . . In too many instances, there was no opportunity for the accused to face his accuser on an equal basis before the bar of public attention. . . .

Candidates for public office were defeated. Their civil rights had been violated, and they paid the penalty.

But the process which the victors used holds within it a danger of which we should all be aware—that technique of character assassination continues. It continues in the press. It continues in the radio. . . .

Critics compared President Truman's "loyalty order" to tactics used by European dictators such as Benito Mussolini and Adolf Hitler to suppress civil rights. (Time & Life Pictures/Getty Images.)

The Dangers of President Truman's Loyalty Order

As a result of this hysteria, this panic against communism, President [Harry S.] Truman has issued a so-called

> I question the wisdom of the methods proposed . . . of determining loyalty, or disloyalty, the provisions for defense against one's accuser.

loyalty order. I believe that President Truman is sincere in issuing such an order. I question the wisdom of the methods proposed, however, . . . of determining loyalty, or disloyalty, the provisions for defense against one's accuser. I do not question the sincerity of the President, nor the desirability of his purpose. I realize that we do not want either Communists or Fascists taking part in confidential positions in our National Government. However, many imminently conservative, reputable people . . . think that certain terms of the order, and the loose method of determining disloyalty, are dangerously broad and lacking in safeguards for the freedom of the individual. The order bestows on the Attorney General arbitrary judicial power regarding civil liberties heretofore reserved to the courts. . . .

It is only the police states that desire the growth of fear in the hearts of their abject subjects. If we continue these practices, people will fear that their jobs will be jeopardized, or that their security will be threatened, or that they will be publicly attacked, and have no means of answering that attack.

They will be afraid to express or to listen to any ideas, whether radical or conservative. The totalitarian states purposely encouraged the growth of fear to control their people. They believe in both tyranny of the body and tyranny of the mind.

Practices and Methods to Guard Against

We know that neither Hitler, [Soviet leader Joseph] Stalin, nor [Italian dictator Benito] Mussolini could rise to power until they had established the pattern for suppressing dissenting ideas. . . . They established it through the suppression of civil liberties and the persecution of the opposition. They created fear, panic, and hysteria in the minds of the people.

These are the things, therefore, that we must guard against. We must guard against the suppression of civil liberties.

We must guard against intemperance and intolerance, whether it be of ideas or of minority groups.

If we do not guard against these insidious practices and methods, our best efforts to combat communism and fascism will fail.

The Need to Retain a Spirit of Democracy

These are the methods which destroy democracy. And when democracy is destroyed, either fascism or communism rushes in to fill the vacuum. . . .

Let me conclude my remarks by reminding you of the oft-quoted statement of [French author and philosopher] Voltaire. "I do not believe a word that you say, but I will defend with my life, if need be, your right to say it."

That is the spirit of democracy, and that attitude of heart and mind must be our guide and compass in the perilous days that lie ahead.

McCarthy Claims Communist Party Members Hold Government Jobs

Joseph McCarthy

Photo on following page: Senator McCarthy claimed that Communist leaders such as Karl Marx, Friedrich Engels, Vladimir Lenin, and Joseph Stalin—seen here on a Soviet propaganda poster—pressed a "religion of immorality." (Getty Images.)

In this 1950 speech to the Republican Women's Club of Wheeling, West Virginia, Joseph McCarthy warns that the United States is in the throes of an ideological war between Communist atheism and Christianity. He contends that the United States has been losing the war and urges Americans to wake up to what is happening and stop the Communists before it is too late. He declares that the biggest threat to the United States comes from within, from Americans who have reaped all the benefits the United States has had to offer. The greatest threat is the State Department and the Secretary of State, which he claims are knowingly harboring more than two hundred members of the Communist Party and allowing them to keep

SOURCE. Joseph McCarthy, "Enemies from Within," Speech at the Ohio County Republican Women's Club of Wheeling, West Virginia, February 9, 1950.

working and shaping US policy. At the time this viewpoint was given, Joseph McCarthy was a senator from Wisconsin.

Ladies and gentlemen, tonight as we celebrate the one hundred forty-first birthday of one of the greatest men in American history, I would like to be able to talk about what a glorious day today is in the history of the world. As we celebrate the birth of this man who with his whole heart and soul hated war, I would like to be able to speak of peace in our time—of war being outlawed—and of world-wide disarmament. These would be truly appropriate things to be able to mention as we celebrate the birthday of Abraham Lincoln.

A Different Kind of War

Five years after a world war has been won, men's hearts should anticipate a long peace—and men's minds should be free from the heavy weight that comes with war. But this is not such a period—for this is not a period of peace. This is a time of "the cold war." This is a time when all the world is split into two vast, increasingly hostile armed camps—a time of a great armament race.

> We are now engaged in a showdown fight . . . a war between two diametrically opposed ideologies.

Today we can almost physically hear the mutterings and rumblings of an invigorated god of war. You can see it, feel it, and hear it all the way from the Indochina hills, from the shores of Formosa, right over into the very heart of Europe itself.

The one encouraging thing is that the "mad moment" has not yet arrived for the firing of the gun or the exploding of the bomb which will set civilization about the final task of destroying itself. There is still a hope for peace if we finally decide that no longer can we safely blind our eyes and close our ears to those facts which are shaping up more and more clearly . . . and that is that we are now engaged in a show-down fight . . . not the usual war between nations for land areas or other material gains, but a war between two diametrically opposed ideologies.

Communism and the West: A Major Moral Difference

The great difference between our western Christian world and the atheistic Communist world is not political, gentlemen, it is moral. For instance, the Marxian idea of confiscating the land and factories and running the entire economy as a single enterprise is momentous. Likewise [Soviet leader Vladimir] Lenin's invention of the one-party police state as a way to make [socialist revolutionary Karl] Marx's idea work is hardly less momentous.

[Soviet leader Joseph] Stalin's resolute putting across of these two ideas, of course, did much to divide the world. With only these differences, however, the east and the west could most certainly still live in peace.

The Communist Religion of Immoralism

The real, basic difference, however, lies in the religion of immoralism . . . invented by Marx, preached feverishly by Lenin, and carried to unimaginable extremes by Stalin. This religion of immoralism, if the Red half of the world triumphs—and well it may, gentlemen—this religion of immoralism will more deeply wound and damage mankind than any conceivable economic or political system.

Karl Marx dismissed God as a hoax, and Lenin and Stalin have added in clear-cut, unmistakable language their resolve that no nation, no people who believe in a god, can exist side by side with their communistic state.

Karl Marx, for example, expelled people from his Communist Party for mentioning such things as love,

Joseph McCarthy: Man on the Move

Joseph McCarthy was that classic American figure, the poor farm boy battling to escape the harsh, sterile dirt farm of his youth, determined to get his share of the American dream. As a youth Joe had tried to make it chicken farming, then tried being a chain-grocery manager. At 20 he quit, crammed four years of high school into one and got into Marquette University, where he made ends meet by jockeying a gas pump, playing poker and coaching boxing. He moved ahead, twisting and turning. At college he switched from engineering to law, in politics he ran for local office as a Democrat and lost, then switched to Republican and won, becoming a Wisconsin circuit court judge. After World War II he made it to the United States Senate.

McCarthy's first three years in the Senate marked him as simply another ambitious young legislator—somewhat prone to use the knee and the elbow, but always with a smile, a wisecrack, the friendly, open look of the American boy playing the get-ahead game, certain everyone understood he meant nothing personal. Joe wasn't mad at anybody, he was just going places. He briefly supported the interests of the sugar and soft drink industries and acquired the Washington nickname of "The Pepsi-Cola Kid," then served the housing interests and got himself called "Water Boy of the Real Estate Lobby." To please his German-American constituents he intruded into a Senate investigation of 43 Nazi SS [secret service] men who had confessed to murdering captured GIs during the Battle of the Bulge and so helped muddy the proceedings of the "Malmédy Massacre" hearings that the murderers were spared. It kept him busy, but it didn't seem to be getting him anywhere.

Then, in Wheeling that February evening as the '50s began, Joe finally caught hold of a star and started his meteoric climb.

SOURCE. This Fabulous Century: 1950–1960, *Volume VI. New York: Time-Life Books, 1970, pp. 117–118.*

justice, humanity or morality. He called this "soulful ravings" and "sloppy sentimentality." . . .

The Time for Battle Is Now

Today we are engaged in a final, all-out battle between communistic atheism and Christianity. The modern champions of communism have selected this as the time, and ladies and gentlemen, the chips are down—they are truly down.

Lest there be any doubt that the time has been chosen, let us go directly to the leader of communism today—Joseph Stalin. Here is what he said—not back in 1928, not before the war, not during the war—but 2 years after the last war was ended: "To think that the Communist revolution can be carried out peacefully, within the framework of a Christian democracy, means one has either gone out of one's mind and lost all normal understanding, or has grossly and openly repudiated the Communist revolution." . . .

> 'When a great democracy is destroyed, it will not be from enemies from without, but rather because of enemies from within.'

Ladies and gentlemen, can there be anyone tonight who is so blind as to say that the war is not on? Can there by anyone who fails to realize that the Communist world has said the time is now? . . . that this is the time for the show-down between the democratic Christian world and the communistic atheistic world?

Unless we face this fact, we shall pay the price that must be paid by those who wait too long.

Soviet Gains and American Defeats

Six years ago, . . . there was within the Soviet orbit, 180,000,000 people. Lined up on the antitotalitarian side there were in the world at that time, roughly 1,625,000,000 people. Today, only six years later, there are 800,000,000 people under the absolute domination of Soviet Russia—an increase of over 400 percent. On our side, the figure has shrunk to around 500,000,000. In other words, in less than six years, the odds have changed from 9 to 1 in our favor to 8 to 5 against us.

This indicates the swiftness of the tempo of Communist victories and American defeats in the cold war. As one of our outstanding historical figures once said, "When a great democracy is destroyed, it will not be from enemies from without, but rather because of enemies from within." . . .

The Threat from Traitors Within the Government

The reason why we find ourselves in a position of impotency is not because our only powerful potential enemy has sent men to invade our shores . . . but rather because of the traitorous actions of those who have been treated so well by this Nation. It has not been the less fortunate, or members of minority groups who have been traitorous to this Nation, but rather those who have had all the benefits that the wealthiest Nation on earth has had to offer . . . the finest homes, the finest college education and the finest jobs in government we can give.

This is glaringly true in the State Department. There the bright young men who are born with silver spoons in their mouths are the ones who have been most traitorous. . . .

I have here in my hand a list of 205 . . . a list of names that were made known to the Secretary of State as being members of the Communist Party and who nevertheless are still working and shaping policy in the State Department. . . .

The Infamy of the Secretary of State

As you know, very recently the Secretary of State proclaimed his loyalty to a man [State Department employee Alger Hiss] guilty of what has always been considered as the most abominable of all crimes—being a traitor to the people who gave him a position of great trust—high treason. . . .

He has lighted the spark which is resulting in a moral uprising and will end only when the whole sorry mess of twisted, warped thinkers are swept from the national scene so that we may have a new birth of honesty and decency in government.

The Politics of Fear Must End

Margaret Chase Smith

In this June 1, 1950, speech to the US Senate and directed in large part to Republican senator Joseph McCarthy, Margaret Chase Smith speaks out against turning the Senate into what she calls a "forum of hate and character assassinations." She accuses some senators of ignoring such basic principles of Americanism as the right to criticize, the right to hold unpopular beliefs, the right to protest, and the right of independent thought. By their actions, she argues, both Democrats and Republicans have played into the Communist tactic of "confuse, divide, and conquer." She contends that the confusion and suspicions bred in the Senate are psychologically dividing the nation and that the Republican Party should bring unity back to the country. At the time of this speech, Margaret Chase Smith was a Republican senator from Maine and the only female member of the US Senate.

Photo on following page: Communist Party members march in Minneapolis in 1939. Critics of the anti-Communist Senate hearings cited the right to hold unpopular beliefs and to protest as basic American principles. (Getty Images.)

SOURCE. Margaret Chase Smith, "A Declaration of Conscience," Speech, June 1, 1950.

Mr. President, I would like to speak briefly and simply about a serious national condition. It is a national feeling of fear and frustration that could result in national suicide and the end of everything that we Americans hold dear. It is a condition that comes from the lack of effective leadership either in the legislative branch or the executive branch of our government.

That leadership is so lacking that serious and responsible proposals are being made that national advisory commissions be appointed to provide such critically needed leadership.

I speak as briefly as possible because too much harm has already been done with irresponsible words of bitterness and selfish political opportunism. I speak as simply as possible because the issue is too great to be obscured by eloquence. I speak simply and briefly in the hope that my words will be taken to heart.

Mr. President, I speak as a Republican. I speak as a woman. I speak as a United States senator. I speak as an American.

The Senate: A Forum of Hate and Character Assassination

The United States Senate has long enjoyed worldwide respect as the greatest deliberative body in the world. But recently that deliberative character has too often been debased to the level of a forum of hate and character assassination sheltered by the shield of congressional immunity.

It is ironical that we senators can in debate in the Senate, directly or indirectly, by any form of words, impute to any American who is not a senator any conduct or motive unworthy or unbecoming an American—and without that non-senator American having any legal redress against us—yet if we say the same thing in the Senate about our colleagues we can be stopped on the grounds of being out of order.

It is strange that we can verbally attack anyone else without restraint and with full protection, and yet we hold ourselves above the same type of criticism here on the Senate floor. Surely the United States Senate is big enough to take self-criticism and self-appraisal. Surely we should be able to take the same kind of character attacks that we "dish out" to outsiders.

A Need to Reevaluate and Change

I think that it is high time for the United States Senate and its members to do some real soul searching and to weigh our consciences as to the manner in which we are performing our duty to the people of America and the manner in which we are using or abusing our individual powers and privileges.

I think that it is high time that we remembered that we have sworn to uphold and defend the Constitution. I think that it is high time that we remembered that the Constitution, as amended, speaks not only of the freedom of speech but also of trial by jury instead of trial by accusation.

Whether it be a criminal prosecution in court or a character prosecution in the Senate, there is little practical distinction when the life of a person has been ruined.

> It is high time that we remembered that the Constitution . . . speaks not only of the freedom of speech but also of trial by jury instead of trial by accusation.

Abuse of the Basic Principles of Americanism

Those of us who shout the loudest about Americanism in making character assassinations are all too frequently those who, by our own words and acts, ignore some of the basic principles of Americanism—

The right to criticize.

The right to hold unpopular beliefs.

The right to protest.

The right of independent thought.

The exercise of these rights should not cost one single American citizen his reputation or his right to a livelihood nor should he be in danger of losing his reputation or livelihood merely because he happens to know someone who holds unpopular beliefs. Who of us does not? Otherwise none of us could call our souls our own. Otherwise thought control would have set in.

The American people are sick and tired of being afraid to speak their minds lest they be politically smeared as "Communists" or "Fascists" by their opponents. Freedom of speech is not what it used to be in America. It has been so abused by some that it is not exercised by others.

The American people are sick and tired of seeing innocent people smeared and guilty people whitewashed. But there have been enough proved cases, such as the *Amerasia* case,[1] the Hiss case,[2] the Coplon case,[3] the Gold case,[4] to cause nationwide distrust and strong suspicion that there may be something to the unproved, sensational accusations.

A Challenge to the Republican Party: A Country Being Divided

As a Republican, I say to my colleagues on this side of the aisle that the Republican party faces a challenge today that is not unlike the challenge which it faced back in Lincoln's day. The Republican party so successfully met that challenge that it emerged from the Civil War as the champion of a united nation—in addition to being a party which unrelentingly fought loose spending and loose programs.

Today our country is being psychologically divided by the confusion and the suspicions that are bred in the United States Senate to spread like cancerous tentacles of "know nothing, suspect everything" attitudes. Today we have a Democratic administration which has developed a mania for loose spending and loose programs. History is repeating itself—and the Republican party again has the opportunity to emerge as the champion of unity and prudence. The record of the present Democratic administration has provided us with sufficient campaign issues without the necessity of resorting to political smears. America is rapidly losing its position as leader of the world simply because the Democratic administration has pitifully failed to provide effective leadership.

Contradictions and Complacency of the Democratic Administration

The Democratic administration has completely confused the American people by its daily contradictory grave warnings and optimistic assurances, which show the people that our Democratic administration has no idea of where it is going.

The Democratic administration has greatly lost the confidence of the American people by its complacency to the threat of communism here at home and the leak of vital secrets to Russia through key officials of the Democratic administration. There are enough proved cases to make this point without diluting our criticism with unproved charges.

Surely these are sufficient reasons to make it clear to the American people that it is time for a change and that a Republican victory is necessary to the security of the country. Surely it is clear that this nation will continue to suffer so long as it is governed by the present ineffective Democratic administration.

> I do not want to see the Republican party ride to political victory on the Four Horsemen of Calumny—Fear, Ignorance, Bigotry, and Smear.

The "Four Horsemen of Calumny" Must Be Avoided

Yet to displace it with a Republican regime embracing a philosophy that lacks political integrity or intellectual honesty would prove equally disastrous to the nation. The nation sorely needs a Republican victory. But I do not want to see the Republican party ride to political victory on the Four Horsemen of Calumny—Fear, Ignorance, Bigotry, and Smear. . . .

I do not want to see the Republican party win that way. While it might be a fleeting victory for the Republican party, it would be a more lasting defeat for the American people. Surely it would ultimately be suicide for the Republican party and the two-party system that has protected our American liberties from the dictatorship of a one-party system.

As members of the minority party, we do not have the primary authority to formulate the policy of our government. But we do have the responsibility of rendering constructive criticism, of clarifying issues, of allaying fears by acting as responsible citizens.

As a woman, I wonder how the mothers, wives, sisters, and daughters feel about the way in which members of their families have been politically mangled in Senate debate—and I use the word "debate" advisedly.

The Irresponsible Sensationalism Must End

> As a United States senator, I am not proud of the way in which the Senate has been made a publicity platform for irresponsible sensationalism.

As a United States senator, I am not proud of the way in which the Senate has been made a publicity platform for irresponsible sensationalism. I am not proud of the reckless abandon in which unproved charges have been hurled from this side of the aisle. I am not proud of the obviously staged, undignified countercharges which have been attempted in retaliation from the other side of the aisle.

I do not like the way the Senate has been made a rendezvous for vilification, for selfish political gain at the sacrifice of individual reputations and national unity. I am not proud of the way we smear outsiders from the floor of the Senate and hide behind the cloak of congressional immunity and still place ourselves beyond criticism on the floor of the Senate.

Unity Must Prevail

As an American, I am shocked at the way Republicans and Democrats alike are playing directly into the Communist design of "confuse, divide, and conquer." As an American, I do not want a Democratic administration "whitewash" or "coverup" any more than I want a Republican smear or witch hunt.

As an American, I condemn a Republican Fascist just as much as I condemn a Democrat Communist. I condemn a Democrat Fascist just as much as I condemn a Republican Communist. They are equally dangerous to you and me and to our country. As an American, I want to see our nation recapture the strength and unity it once had when we fought the enemy instead of ourselves.

A Declaration of Conscience

It is with these thoughts that I have drafted what I call a Declaration of Conscience. I am gratified that the senator from New Hampshire [Charles W. Tobey], the senator from Vermont [George D. Aiken], the senator from Oregon [Wayne L. Morse], the senator from New York [Irving M. Ives], the senator from Minnesota [Edward J. Thyne] and the senator from New Jersey [Robert C. Hendrickson] have concurred in that declaration and have authorized me to announce their concurrence.

The declaration reads as follows:

1. We are Republicans. But we are Americans first. It is as Americans that we express our concern with the growing confusion that threatens the security and stability of our country. Democrats and Republicans alike have contributed to that confusion.

2. The Democratic administration has initially created the confusion by its lack of effective leadership, by its contradictory grave warnings and optimistic assurances, by its complacency to the threat of communism here at home, by its oversensitiveness to rightful criticism, by its petty bitterness against its critics.

3. Certain elements of the Republican party have materially added to this confusion in the hopes of riding the Republican party to victory through the selfish political exploitation of fear, bigotry, ignorance, and intolerance. There are enough mistakes of the Democrats for Republicans to criticize constructively without resorting to political smears.

4. To this extent, Democrats and Republicans alike have unwittingly, but undeniably, played directly into the Communist design of "confuse, divide, and conquer."

5. It is high time that we stopped thinking politically as Republicans and Democrats about elections and started thinking patriotically as Americans about national security based on individual freedom. It is high time that we all stopped being tools and victims of totalitarian techniques—techniques that, if continued here unchecked, will surely end what we have come to cherish as the American way of life.

Notes

1. Spy case that centered around classified government documents found in the New York office of a pro-Communist journal.
2. Case of a State Department employee, Alger Hiss, accused of being a Russian spy.
3. Case of a Justice Department employee, Judy Coplon, caught passing classified files to a Russian agent employed by the United Nations.
4. Case of a chemist, Harry Gold, who traveled all over the United States collecting atomic secrets to pass to the Soviet Union.

The Rosenbergs Did Not Get a Fair Trial

National Committee to Reopen the Rosenberg Case

In the following viewpoint, the National Committee to Reopen the Rosenberg Case argues that Julius and Ethel Rosenberg were unfairly tried and convicted. It asserts, among other things, that (1) the Rosenbergs were not sentenced based on what the trial or the jury had established, but on the personal, imagined beliefs of a biased judge who tainted the judicial process; (2) the prosecution knowingly used unsupported and perjured testimony; (3) the government knew Ethel Rosenberg was not guilty but used the threat of her conviction and the death sentence to convince her husband to confess or incriminate others; and that (4) the Rosenbergs were tried under the wrong law so that the death penalty could be used. The National Committee to Reopen the Rosenberg Case was founded in 1960. Its mission has been to reopen the Rosenberg case legally, legislatively, and politically.

SOURCE. National Committee to Reopen the Rosenberg Case, "Case for the Defense," 2002. Reproduced by permission.

*T*he Rosenbergs were sentenced for crimes for which they were not tried. They were neither tried nor convicted of treason or any form of espionage.

The Issue of Charges

In effect the Rosenbergs were denied the *right of confrontation*. . . . This right guarantees that a defendant will be confronted with the charges against him and will be given the opportunity to reply in a court of law! [Judge Irving R.] Kaufman's charges were first voiced seven days *after* the trial had ended. The defendants never had an opportunity to reply.

The Trial Record shows that Judge Kaufman made it clear to the jurors that the charge against the defendants was only for *conspiring* to commit espionage, and not for *passing classified material.* Seven days after the jury convicted them with that understanding, Kaufman said "*. . . death . . . for putting the A-bomb in the hands of the Russians*" and for causing the war in Korea and the 50,000 GI casualties. Yet the indictment under which they were tried contained no charge that they had ever passed classified information. Thus they were being punished for crimes for which they never had a trial.

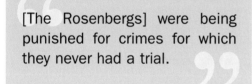

[The Rosenbergs] were being punished for crimes for which they never had a trial.

A Sentence Based on Personal Beliefs

From Kaufman's sentencing speech: "*. . . millions of . . . innocent people may pay the price of your treason.*" A charge of treason is the only crime defined in the U.S. Constitution. Treason consists of aiding the *enemy* in time of war. (Whereas the accusation against the Rosenbergs was helping a *wartime ally*.) Its successful prosecution requires the corroboration of at least two independent witnesses describing at least one overt act of treason. Nothing like this was either charged or proven at the Rosenberg trial.

Thus the Rosenbergs were sentenced *not* on the basis of what the trial or the jury had established, but on Kaufman's personal, imagined beliefs that the defendants committed treason by passing classified material that had caused the war in Korea; 50,000 American casualties; and the death of untold millions.

Accomplice and Perjured Testimony

The prosecution used accomplice (not independently corroborated) and perjured testimony. The Rosenbergs were convicted primarily on the testimony of self-confessed co-conspirators: the Greenglasses and Harry Gold.

Accomplice testimony, by its very nature, has to be less trustworthy than that of a neutral, disinterested person. The main witnesses against the Rosenbergs were Ethel's brother David Greenglass and his wife Ruth. The government had evidence against these witnesses which could have had them sentenced to death. With this threat hanging over them, and with the government's aid (and advice from their lawyers), they perjured themselves. The FBI and the prosecutors arranged this. One example is the perjured testimony of David Greenglass regarding the typing of David's notes by Ethel.

Another is the recognition phrase "*I come from Julius.*" This was an important part of the government's case because it seemingly tied Harry Gold to the Rosenbergs. (Gold testified that he had neither met nor heard of the Rosenbergs.) This phrase, "*I come from Julius,*" was supposedly used when Harry Gold met the Greenglasses in Albuquerque, New Mexico. In fact it was concocted a few months preceding the trial during a December 28, 1950, meeting in prison between the FBI, Gold, and Greenglass. . . .

The testimony of the Greenglasses was coerced under the threat of death: "cooperative or die." Furthermore,

their testimonies and that of Harry Gold included last minute changes that contradicted earlier statements made to the FBI, grand jury, or prosecution before the trial began. Naturally, these earlier statements were never mentioned in court. . . .

The Pretense of Atomic Secrets

There were no atomic secrets that David Greenglass had the knowledge to transmit. The Commander of the Manhattan Project, General Leslie Groves, and an Atomic Energy Commission spokesman, James Beckerly, have agreed that the crime was fictitious. . . .

The Bulletin of Atomic Scientists, and leading atomic scientists . . . maintained that there was no such thing as a secret formula or recipe for making the A-bomb. . . .

Dr. Phillip Morrison, co-holder of a patent on the atomic bomb: ". . . *The entire testimony of Greenglass concerning the bomb is confused and imprecise . . . he had neither the scientific background . . . nor was he closely associated with the technical aspects of the project. . . . The drawing [Greenglass' sketch] was completely insufficient and could not be used for any construction purposes. . . ."*

Nine months after the Rosenbergs were electrocuted, Atomic Energy Commission spokesman James Beckerly was quoted in the *New York Times*, March 17, 1954, to the effect that is was time Americans "*stopped kidding ourselves*" about the atom bomb having been stolen from us by spies. "*Atom bombs and Hydrogen bombs,*" he said, "*are not matters that can be stolen and transmitted in the form of information.*" That statement actually refuted the basic charge in the Rosenberg Case and the so-called justification for the outrageous sentences. . . .

Judicial Interference and Lack of Impartiality

Judge Kaufman contaminated the judicial process. This occurred before, during, and after the trial.

Photo on previous page: Last rites are read over the grave of a US soldier in Korea in 1950. Julius and Ethel Rosenberg were executed for causing the deaths of 50,000 US soldiers in Korea even though they were convicted only on conspiracy charges. (**Getty Images.**)

Any semblance of judicial impartiality ended *before* the start of the trial. Judge Kaufman, a known hater of Communists, actively campaigned to be assigned to this case. An FBI document . . . indicates that part of the reason that he was chosen to adjudicate this case was that he assured officials in the Justice Department that he would impose the death sentence if warranted. Indeed this same document shows that this kind of unlawful *ex parte* communication, where a judge discusses the case with the prosecution but without the presence of the defense, continued throughout the trial.

His strong bias is next demonstrated during the jury selection process. During the trial, Judge Kaufman behaved as if he was an additional member of the prosecution team. . . .

> [Judge] Kaufman made extraordinary efforts to expedite the executions and to frustrate the appeal process.

FBI documents show that Kaufman made extraordinary efforts to expedite the executions and to frustrate the appeal process by denying *habeas corpus* relief without hearing, by communicating secretly with members of the prosecution staff, the FBI and through them, with the Department of Justice.

For example: the record reveals that the last application of the Rosenbergs to set aside their sentences was made in June, 1953. It came to be heard before Judge Kaufman and was summarily denied *without affording any evidentiary hearing.* The record also reveals that prior to the time the motion was even filed, subject matter of the notion was secretly discussed at a meeting between [FBI director J. Edgar] Hoover and Judge Kaufman in May of 1953. The prosecution thereafter briefed him as to the issues that might be raised before the target motion was made, thus permitting the summary denial.

And Kaufman's interference did not stop there. Even after the executions took place his need for vindication continued for over 20 years. He used the FBI to register distress over ongoing legal efforts to free Morton Sobell (co-defendant); any changes in the law which tended to weaken the legal underpinnings of the trial and appellate process; and all hearings in Congress and other efforts to have the case reopened. . . .

Use and Role of the McCarran Act

The McCarran Act was used to prejudice the jury selection process and the Rosenbergs' Testimony.

The McCarran Internal Security Act of 1950 was passed just months *after* the Rosenbergs were arrested. . . . The Act held that all members of the Communist Party, and all members of 100 organizations listed by the Attorney General as *Communist Front* organizations (over half of a million Americans), are in effect agents of the Soviet Union.

Kaufman was one of the first judges to utilize the McCarran Act in the courtroom. In eliminating potential jurors, Kaufman not only used the criteria of membership in the list of organizations specified by the McCarran Act, but *added* several "communist front" organizations of his own choosing. He then further extended dismissal to include *former members* and *friends and family* of any members of these organizations. Thus, thousands of potential jurors with liberal or progressive viewpoints were eliminated from consideration.

When the Rosenbergs were on the witness stand and asked if they had been members of the Communist Party, they took the 5th Amendment. Because of the McCarran Act, the jurors were then able to form the equation:

5th Amendment = Communist = Soviet agent = spy.

This had to prejudice the jury against the defendants. No longer could the jury be objective when considering their testimony. . . .

> *Ethel's death sentence was a 'lever' against Julius.*

Targeting Ethel Rosenberg

Ethel's death sentence was a "lever" against Julius. The government knew she was innocent.

On December 5, 2001, David Greenglass admitted on the nationally televised *60 Minutes II* that he had committed perjury during the Rosenberg trial, and was encouraged to do so by special assistant prosecutor Roy Cohn. . . . Unknown to David at the time of the trial was that without this crucial perjured testimony, the government had no case against his sister Ethel. If not for this testimony (and the corroborating testimony of his wife Ruth), Ethel Rosenberg might not have been convicted.

Ethel Rosenberg had not been a target for FBI investigation until it became apparent that Julius, who was still insisting on his innocence, would not confess nor implicate others. Her arrest on August 11, 25 days after Julius', was intended as a lever to elicit testimony from her husband. Before the Joint Congressional Committee on Atomic Energy, assistant U.S. Attorney Myles J. Lane said: ". . . *the only thing that will break this man Rosenberg is the prospect of . . . getting the chair, plus that if we can convict his wife, too and give her . . . 25 to 30 years.*" The problem for [US attorney Irving H.] Saypol was how to convict Ethel. On what evidence? The prosecuting team had to overcome their lack of proof of Ethel's guilt. When reviewing her work experience, the FBI noted that she had been a typist. Perhaps she was instrumental in the typing of A-bomb secrets? That's it. On re-questioning, Ruth Greenglass stated that Ethel, in September of 1945, had typed up David's espionage data. (Ethel denied this on the witness stand.) Ruth's testimony implicating Ethel as a spy was developed 10 days before the trial.

David Greenglass quickly confirmed his wife's new evidence: Ethel typed A-bomb secrets. However,

> FBI documents show that the Supreme Court was compromised by the Justice Department.

when questioned six months earlier by Lane about the September 1945 meeting, David Greenglass denied that Ethel was even there. . . .

Judicial Agreements and Improprieties

FBI documents show that the Supreme Court was compromised by the Justice Department.

It is Monday, June 15, 1953; just three days before the scheduled electrocutions of the Rosenbergs. It is also the last day the Supreme Court would meet before adjourning for its summer vacation. In a highly improper "gentleman's agreement," the nine justices agreed that *any new motions, regardless of merit*, pertaining to the Rosenberg case, will not be considered. . . .

In meetings documented by the FBI, Justices [Fred M.] Vinson and [Robert H.] Jackson privately met with the Attorney General [Herbert] Brownell to discuss what actions would be taken if Justices [William O.] Douglas or [Felix] Frankfurter were to break the gentleman's agreement. They knew that Douglas or Frankfurter was considering a petition by [attorneys] Fyke Farmer and Daniel Marshall pertaining to the Rosenberg case. On Tuesday, June 16, Vinson, Jackson, and Brownell agreed that if Douglas submitted a stay of execution in order to have the Farmer-Marshall petition considered, they would immediately convene a special session of the court to overturn the stay. Furthermore, at Brownell's suggestion, Chief Justice Vinson agreed to meet privately with Douglas and try to convince him not to decide the merits of the new motion himself, but to submit the motion for consideration in conference. . . .

A Low Point of Judicial Conduct

Meetings of this type (between Brownell and Vinson) are called *ex parte communication*, and are strictly forbidden by the canons of ethics for both judges and lawyers. Any meeting between judge and prosecutor, pertaining to a case at hand, which does not also include a member of the defense, is unethical and improper.

The repercussions of these meetings were to result in perhaps a low point of judicial conduct by the court. Vinson actually met with Douglas and tried to persuade him to not consider the merits of the Farmer-Marshall petition himself. After this failed, and Douglas issued a stay on June 17th, *the ex* parte Brownell-Jackson-Vinson contingency plan was put into motion.

> The Rosenbergs, who were tried under the Espionage Act of 1917, should have been tried under the Atomic Energy Act of 1946.

On June 18th, for only the *third time* in its history, the Supreme Court was reconvened after adjournment for vacation. (Neither the defense attorneys nor Justice Douglas were notified that this meeting was to take place.) And for the *first time in its history*, a stay by one of the judges was vacated by the other members of the court. Supreme Court scholars are still unclear as to whether such an action is even legal. . . .

The Issue of the Death Penalty

The Rosenbergs were tried under the wrong law in order to facilitate the use of the death penalty.

Fyke Farmer and Daniel Marshall had filed *amicus curiae* ["friends of the court"] petitions with Judge Kaufman, the Appellate Court, and the Supreme Court. They contended that the Rosenbergs, who were tried under the Espionage Act of 1917, should have been tried under the Atomic Energy Act of 1946. The death sentence could only be imposed under the 1946 act if two conditions were met. The first is that the prosecution had to demonstrate that the defendants' actions had "harmed the United States," not just that they had "aided a foreign power" (as is true under the 1917 act). Secondly, the death penalty could be imposed only upon recommendation by the jury.

A Possible Conflict Unresolved

Farmer and Marshall argued that the charge against the Rosenbergs was conspiracy to commit espionage during the period from June 1944 through June 16, 1950. And that conspiracy is a *continuing* offense. It did not matter when the Rosenberg conspiracy began as long as it continued past August 1, 1946, the date the Atomic Energy Act was enacted. The indictment said that the so called conspiracy lasted into 1950, removing any constitutional argument that the 1946 act did not apply. The government applied and emphasized post 1946 conduct in convicting the Rosenbergs. Much of the testimony dealt with events after August 1, 1946. . . .

This was the first time that the Supreme Court had ever been asked to consider a possible conflict involving the application of the 1917 Espionage Act and the Atomic Energy Act of 1946. It is customary that when deciding an important point of law such as this . . . that the Court would have to either refer the case to a lower court or itself decide on the issues at hand. After all, how could the Court make a just and fair decision if it does not review the case? Yet, this is exactly what happened. The Supreme Court decided on the merits of the Farmer/ Marshall motion without ever reviewing the Rosenberg case or remanding it to a lower court.

McCarthy Has Been Unfairly Condemned

Ray Wannall

In the following viewpoint, Ray Wannall argues that Senator Joseph McCarthy did his country a service when he publicly charged in 1950 that Communist agents had infiltrated the US government in general and the State Department in particular. Wannall maintains that McCarthy's charges were, if anything, understated and that his anti-Communist crusade demonstrated his love for and support of his country. Evidence of espionage existed before McCarthy began his crusade. In the late 1940s dozens of traitorous Americans in government service were named and the House Committee on Un-American Activities reported that Communist espionage rings were at work in US executive agencies. Wannall contends that McCarthy and his actions have been misrepresented by an unjust, anti-McCarthy campaign initiated by liberals and Communists and perpetuated by establishment historians, liberal journalists, and politicians. Ray Wannall is a former assistant director of the Federal Bureau of Investigation.

SOURCE. Ray Wannall, "The Red Road to 'McCarthyism,'" *Human Events*, April 12, 1996. Reproduced by permission.

When in December 1954, the U.S. Senate voted to condemn Sen. Joseph R. McCarthy (R.-Wis.)—not for falsely accusing anyone of communism, but for criticisms he had made of an army general and a Senate elections subcommittee—liberals, as well as Communists, were overjoyed. Their vilification of the man began following the senator's public charge in 1950 that our government, specifically the State Department, had been infiltrated by Communists. There has been a highly successful "Joe McCarthy for President of Hades" campaign ever since.

The National Security Agency's release of the "Venona" documents [in 1995], intercepted communications of Soviet KGB [Committee for State Security] officers in the United States to their bosses in Moscow, suggests that McCarthy's charges of government infiltration understated the reality.

> " At the close of World War II, world communism adopted a new strategy that made the United States its 'main enemy.' "

The United States: Soviet Enemy and Target

At the close of World War II, world communism adopted a new strategy that made the United States its "main enemy." In the immediate postwar period, the Soviets had conquered Eastern Europe, including Romania, Bulgaria, Hungary and Poland. In 1948, Czechoslovakia was subverted, the Soviets' having drawn what [British prime minister] Winston Churchill described as an "iron curtain" across the face of Europe. The Soviets blockaded Berlin on April 1, 1948, hoping to dominate that city and eventually all of Germany. In the Far East, the Soviets were helping [Chinese Communist leader] Mao Tse-tung topple the anti-Communist government in China.

But the Soviets had also clearly targeted this country as well. Indeed, against the backdrop of what was happening in Europe and Asia, Elizabeth Terrell Bentley and Whittaker Chambers, both of whom were defected couriers for the Soviet intelligence service, testified before the House Committee on Un-American Activities (HCUA) during the summer of 1948. They named more than three dozen traitorous Americans who had infiltrated numerous U.S. Government agencies, where, on

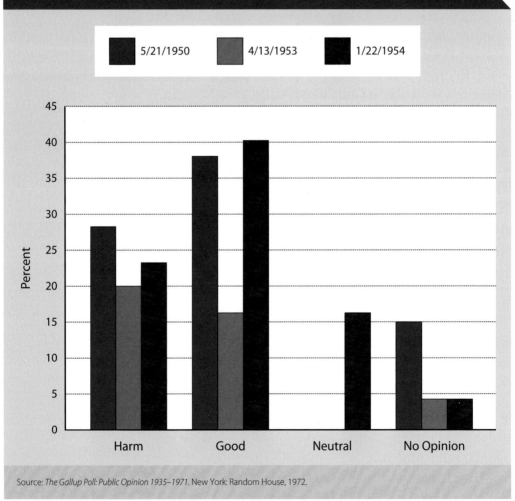

PUBLIC OPINION ON WHETHER MCCARTHY'S ACCUSATIONS WERE DOING THE UNITED STATES MORE HARM THAN GOOD

Legend: 5/21/1950, 4/13/1953, 1/22/1954

Source: *The Gallup Poll: Public Opinion 1935–1971*. New York: Random House, 1972.

behalf of the Soviets, these Americans were influencing policy and stealing vital secrets.

At least two dozen of them occupied sensitive positions in the Departments of State and Treasury, and one even served as an assistant to the President. Among them were Alger Hiss, Harry Dexter White, Soloman Adler and Lauchlin Currie.

Communist Sympathizers in Influential Government Jobs

Hiss, as a senior State Department official, was at the right hand of President Franklin D. Roosevelt when Eastern Europe was sold out at the Yalta Conference and was one of the architects of the United Nations. White, as assistant secretary of the Treasury, had full responsibility for all Treasury Department matters relating to foreign relations, as well as economic and financial affairs.

Adler, who served under White, was Treasury's man in Ch'ung-ch'ing, China. After being cleared in a series of security and loyalty investigations, Adler resigned and went back to China to spend the rest of his career working for the Chinese Communists.

Currie, administrative assistant to FDR [US president Franklin D. Roosevelt], was described by Whittaker Chambers as a "fellow traveler [sympathizer]." But testifying under oath, Bentley, who also had served the Soviets later than Chambers, said that Currie not only possessed inside information on government policy, but also had even once relayed to the Soviets word that the United States was on the verge of breaking their code. The Venona documents have now verified the truthfulness of Chambers' and Bentley's testimonies.

Communist Espionage Rings at Work

On July 20, 1948, 12 U.S. Communist Party (CPUSA) leaders were indicted, charged with conspiracy to teach and advocate the violent overthrow of the U.S. government in violation of the Smith Act [Alien Registration Act of 1940]. [William Z.] Foster, one of those indicted, was not tried because of a heart condition. The remaining eleven were found guilty 15 months later. With this decision, the jury upheld the charges that the Communist Party was a criminal conspiracy, that it advocated violent overthrow of the U.S. government and that it took its orders from Moscow.

The HCUA issued a report on August 28, 1948, which concluded:

> During the late war and since then, there have been numerous Communist espionage rings at work in our executive agencies which have worked with and through the American Communist Party and its agents to relay to Russia vital information essential to our national defense and security. Russian Communists have worked hand in hand with American Communists in these espionage activities.

In January 1949, the attorney general urged Congress to pass "drastic new anti-espionage laws."

Two Reasons for McCarthy to Launch His Anti-Communist Crusade

"FBI Director J. Edgar Hoover estimated that there were 54,174 Communist Party members in the United States and 10 times as many sympathizers."

Nearly three weeks before Sen. McCarthy's charge that the State Department had been infiltrated by Communists, there were two occurrences that undoubtedly bolstered his determination to go ahead with his anti-Communist crusade: 1) On Jan. 21, 1950, Alger Hiss was found guilty by a New York federal jury of perjury in denying under oath charges by Whittaker Chambers that Hiss had engaged in Soviet espionage; 2) Testifying on February 3 before a Senate Committee on Appropriations subcom-

Soviet forces set up blockades of rubble in Berlin in 1948 separating the eastern portion of the city from the sections controlled by the United States, Britain, and France. Many Americans interpreted this and other Soviet actions as acts of aggression. (**Associated Press.**)

mittee, FBI Director J. Edgar Hoover estimated that there were 54,174 Communist Party members in the United States and 10 times as many sympathizers. (This constituted a ready-made nucleus of McCarthy critics and vilifiers once the senator launched his anti-Communist crusade.)

Director Hoover told the subcommittee members that 48% of the membership of the Communist Party was in the "basic industry" of the country. "In this manner, they would be able to sabotage essential industry in vital defense areas in the event of a national emergency." He also pointed out that through increased activities the Communist Party had "endeavored to exploit youth, veterans, civil rights, foreign nationality, the press, radio,

Murrow vs. McCarthy

On the evening of March 9, 1954, [CBS's newsmagazine and documentary series] *See It Now* tackled Senator [Joseph] McCarthy when he was at his most powerful and exposed him as a fraud.

[The host of the show, broadcast journalist] Edward R. Murrow said at the end: "This is no time for men who oppose Senator McCarthy's methods to keep silent. We can deny our heritage and our history, but we cannot escape responsibility for the result. There is no way for a citizen of a republic to abdicate his responsibilities."

It would be difficult to exaggerate the courage Murrow displayed on this program, or the malice it aroused. Merely by saying at the end of it, "I want to associate myself with every word just spoken by Ed Murrow," Don Hollenbeck, the network's regular 11 P.M. newscaster, touched off a Hearst crusade against him that ended in his suicide. CBS—which was administering loyalty oaths to its own employees and hiring ex-FBI agents to investigate them—was appalled. (Murrow, now a director of the network, described the reaction of his colleagues at their next meeting as, "Good show. Sorry you did it.") McCarthy himself said scornfully that he hadn't seen it: "I never listen to the extreme left-wing, bleeding heart elements of radio and TV." He wouldn't deign to reply on the air, so CBS gave the time to Vice President Nixon, who spent it begging McCarthy to follow the Republican party line.

SOURCE. *William Manchester,* The Glory and the Dream: A Narrative History of America 1932–1972. *Boston: Little, Brown and Company, 1973, p. 631.*

television, the motion picture industry, educational, political, women and labor groups."

More Evidence of Communist Infiltration

Following McCarthy's ["Enemies from Within"] West Virginia speech [in 1950], more evidence emerged about how the Communists were infiltrating our government. Here are just a few examples:

- In January 1951, Elizabeth Bentley testified at the trial of William W. Remington, charging that while he was employed by the War Production Board, he gave her secret information for transmission to the USSR [Union of Soviet Socialist Republics]. During her testimony, she said that she learned in advance the date of D-Day [the 1944 invasion of Normandy] in Europe from William Ludwig Ullman, an officer in the Army Air Corps.

- Julius and Ethel Rosenberg, along with Morton Sobell, on March 29, 1951, were found guilty of engaging in Soviet espionage.

- Testifying Aug. 2, 1951, before the Senate Internal Security Subcommittee, Mrs. Hede Massing, a former Communist espionage agent, stated that she had recruited as spies in 1934 two State Department officials, Noel H. Field and Laurence Duggan. She said that Alger Hiss had competed with her in an effort to get Field for his own spy ring, but that she had won.

- The following month, a former Communist Party official, John Lautner, testified in a New York trial that in 1949 Communist Party students were taught that "in case of a war against the Soviet Union, the task of every Communist would be to wage a struggle, if necessary, against our own imperialist government."

On Target: McCarthy's Concern About Infiltration in the State Department

The recently released papers of the Venona project underscore the fact that our government was massively riddled with Americans in high-ranking positions who were tilting policy to serve Soviet ends and engaging in espionage, including sharing our atomic secrets with Stalinist Russia.

Sen. McCarthy dramatically brought attention to this incredible story, and he had been right to be especially concerned about the State Department. Not only had the department been infiltrated by such high-ranking officials as Hiss, but also, according to former Deputy Assistant Secretary of State J. Anthony Panuch, thousands of "unscreened personnel," i.e., unscreened as to whether they were Communists and their sympathizers or as to whether they could be blackmailed, had been merged into the department from other agencies following World War II.

Nevertheless, McCarthy was thoroughly condemned and vilified by a broad spectrum of those on the left side of the political spectrum. The Communist party publication *Political Affairs* in June 1953 carded an article titled "The Anatomy of McCarthyism," which placed the Party in the vanguard of the anti-McCarthy forces and constituted an organized movement against the beleaguered warrior.

The Big Lie: Anti-McCarthy Message

The senator was vilified by means of the "technique of the Big Lie," and the anti-McCarthy campaign gathered steam as politicians, left-wing professors and media elements joined the assault.

Political Affairs adorned the word "McCarthyism" with all sorts of vulgar epithets. McCarthyism was "a method of terror" and "an instrument designed to soften up and prepare the ground for fascism." He was "the heir apparent of [Nazi Minister of Propaganda Joseph] Goebbels, who presumed to speak as the voice of America." The Communist publication declared, "The immediate and broadest rallying ground in the struggle for democratic liberties is the fight against McCarthyism."

In the wake of what we knew about communism and how thoroughly our government had been penetrated by Soviet agents before Joe McCarthy exploded onto the political scene, it is difficult to understand how so many Americans rallied to the anti-McCarthy cause, or how the term "McCarthyism" has taken on such a derisive tone.

> It is difficult to understand how so many Americans rallied to the anti-McCarthy cause, or how the term 'McCarthyism' has taken on such a derisive tone.

"McCarthyism": Unwanted Smears by the Left

Because of the virulent, anti-McCarthy message spread by establishment historians, liberal journalists and the hard left, the record does not always precisely portray what McCarthy did or the reasons behind his actions. Those who coined the term "McCarthyism" have succeeded in besmirching the name and reputation of a staunch and sincere, if somewhat overzealous, adversary of the Communists, a man whose love of country and support of all it represents are beyond reproach.

Many who assailed this ex-Marine were apprehensive about what he might reveal concerning them and their friends and they reacted with fury. They claimed that those who practiced "McCarthyism" were engaged in unspeakable smears and "guilt by association." By associating the name of McCarthy or the "McCarthy era" with actions, rhetoric and policies they opposed, the senator's foes, along with their ideological heirs, have become the foremost practitioners of what they call McCarthyism.

McCarthyism Was Not About Soviet Spies

William Pfaff

In the following viewpoint, William Pfaff declares that there are two myths about Joe McCarthy: (1) that he was an "American-style fascist crushing liberal forces," and (2) that McCarthyism had to do with spies and Soviet agents. McCarthy's campaign, argues Pfaff, did not target spies or Soviet agents; it targeted US government employees who had signed petitions or joined organizations expressing Communist views. McCarthy was simply anti-liberal—branded a menace to civil liberties and democracy by some—intent on stifling and censoring what he viewed as liberal teachings and opinion. According to Pfaff, McCarthy got in the way of those trying to wage a serious fight against Communists in the United States and ended up helping the Soviet effort by discrediting anti-communism. William Pfaff is a columnist for the *International Herald Tribune* and the author of numerous books on American foreign policy, international relations, and contemporary history.

Photo on following page: Henry A. Wallace ran for US president in 1948 as a member of the Progressive Party in an important bid to influence American policy with Communist ideas. (**Associated Press.**)

SOURCE. William Pfaff, "McCarthyism Revised? No, It Wasn't About Soviet Spies," *International Herald Tribune*, October 29, 1998. Reproduced by permission.

A revisionist view of McCarthyism is making its way in newspapers and academic circles. Certain writers in London as well as in the United States suggest that despite all, Joseph McCarthy's campaign against Communists and fellow travelers [Communist sympathizers] in the 1950s was justified by Soviet penetration of the U.S. government.

Facts Scholars Should Have Known

The *New York Times* recently [October 18, 1998] ran an article called "Rethinking McCarthyism, if Not McCarthy." It quoted evidence from newly opened archives of the [former Communist agency the] Comintern and the Soviet government which shows that there were indeed Communist spies and agents of political influence in the United States during and after World War II. It said this evidence discredits "many icons of the old left," such as [convicted spy] Julius Rosenberg, [former State Department employee accused of spying for the Soviet Union] Alger Hiss and the "epic" interpretation of the [1936–1939] Spanish civil war. Only very young or very innocent scholars would think it a revelation that Rosenberg and Hiss were spies or that the Soviet Union played a sinister and politically exploitative role in the Spanish civil war. [Authors] Ernest Hemingway, Arthur Koestler and George Orwell, among others, attested to the latter. Where have these scholars been?

Two Common Myths About McCarthy

There are two myths about McCarthy. The first is that he was an American-style fascist crushing liberal forces. That was the Communist myth, still influential. The second, that of the senator's defenders, is that McCarthyism had to do with spies and Soviet agents.

It was not about spies. It was about people who had been Communist Party members, or who had expressed pro-Communist sympathies. The senator's targets were people in the U.S. government who in the 1930s or 1940s had signed petitions or joined committees expressing such views.

He hounded the State Department with constantly shifting "lists" of alleged Communists or pro-Communists. He went after the U.S. Information Agency. Some of the people fired after having been abandoned by cowardly superiors elsewhere in government were picked up by the CIA [Central Intelligence Agency], then considered the most open-minded and liberal government agency.

> His was a haphazard and totally opportunistic campaign to suppress opinions and to censor what was thought and taught in the United States.

A Messy and Unethical Campaign of Censorship

The senator got books censored in libraries. He persecuted scholars with government connections. He went after the Council on Foreign Relations and Harvard. His chosen targets were the institutions of the liberal Eastern "Establishment." He was in part the product of social resentment.

His was a haphazard and totally opportunistic campaign to suppress opinions and to censor what was thought and taught in the United States. This had nothing to do with files in the Soviet archives.

He was a hail-fellow-well-met demagogue, not too intelligent, onto a good thing, who liked the bottle which eventually got him.

Communist Efforts in the United States in the 1940s

McCarthyism came four years too late to influence the most important Communist bid to influence U.S. domestic politics, the party's revival of the Progressive Party in order to run [former US president] Franklin Roosevelt's

The US Senate Condemns McCarthy

On December 2, 1954, amid cat-calls and bitter laughter from die-hard McCarthy supporters, the senators rendered their verdict.

By sixty-seven to twenty-two, the United States Senate voted to condemn Joe McCarthy's conduct for having been "contrary to Senate tradition."

This final act of political judgment might seem inevitable in retrospect. It wasn't. There was enough intrigue and high-stakes, behind-the-scenes maneuvers in the days leading to the final vote to provide grist for a host of Washington potboilers. Though McCarthy had lost forever the support of the American majority, he retained the passionate backing of bitter-end Republican conservatives who had fought a last-ditch battle to save him. The final vote reflected that ideological division: every Democrat present and voting . . . plus the sole Independent . . . voted against McCarthy. By contrast, Republican senators were split down the middle. . . . Right-wing forces stayed with McCarthy, the more progressive eastern GOP wing opposed him. Only three senators failed to vote. . . .

Nor did the judgment take place without more dramatic encounters and fierce in-fighting, both public and private. No sooner had the votes been tallied than the bitter-enders launched an effort to discredit the proceedings and diminish the meaning of what had taken place. The right-wing Republican Styles Bridges arose to inquire whether the word "censure" appeared in the solution on which the senators had just voted. If so, it was incorrect. . . . Vice President Richard Nixon . . . hurriedly struck the word "censure" from the title. . . .

More jeers from the bitter-enders. . . . At this point, [Senator William] Fulbright . . . asked the parliamentarian to provide a dictionary. He read to his colleagues the definition of both "censure" and "condemn." . . . They were synonymous. Case closed.

The Senate's condemnation left many of McCarthy's transgressions unanswered. It was not close to being definitive. But it was enough to inflict a fatal blow.

SOURCE. *Haynes Johnson,* The Age of Anxiety: McCarthyism to Terrorism. *New York: Harcourt, 2005, pp. 440–442.*

former vice president, Henry Wallace, for the presidency against Harry Truman. Wallace won a million votes. The *New Republic* was the voice of the Wallace campaign. Mr. Wallace was firmly endorsed by the *Nation*.

In those days there was a struggle going on to control certain unions in the United States and dominate influential magazines and political groups. In 1948, liberal anti-Communists fought the Progressive Party and the Wallace candidacy. They founded a new organization, Americans for Democratic Action, to do so.

> McCarthy was a nuisance and obstacle to the effort to conduct a serious struggle against the Communists in the United States.

Other liberal anti-Communists painstakingly out-organized and out-witted the Communist faction trying to take control of the World War II veterans' organization, the American Veterans Committee.

The Menace of McCarthy

Many of the people most active in this fight came from the predominantly Jewish Social Democratic movement, influential in certain big New York unions. The Social Democrats had a weekly, *The New Leader*, which for years was the principal serious and informed anti-Communist journal in the United States. McCarthy hated liberals and considered Social Democrats indistinguishable from Communists.

The Association of Catholic Trade Unions fought the Communist effort to control New York's longshoremen and certain other unions. It was supported by the lay Catholic magazine *Commonweal*, which attacked the Catholic McCarthy as a menace to civil liberties and democracy.

McCarthy was a nuisance and obstacle to the effort to conduct a serious struggle against the Communists in the United States, at a time when the Soviet Union was attempting to enlarge its influence over the left in Europe, and the Cold War was growing colder.

Many, at the time, believed that he was the best political asset the Soviet Union had in those years. The effect of McCarthyism was to discredit anti-Communism.

A New McCarthyism Is on the Rise

People for the American Way

In the following viewpoint, People for the American Way attributes the rise of a new McCarthyism to Republican members of Congress and other party officials, right-wing cable television personalities, some radio hosts, religious right leaders, other right-wing organizations, and their phony "grassroots" campaigns. These individuals and groups, contends People for the American Way, use the same language and tactics commonly used by Senator Joseph McCarthy in the 1950s—character assassination, guilt by association, smear campaigns—to lead people to believe that the administration and its allies, congressional Democratic leaders, intellectuals, "elites," and others within the country are threatening national interests. Like McCarthy, they accuse President Barack Obama's administration and congressional Democratic leaders of being Communists, socialists, or fascists who want to destroy the United States. People for the American Way is a politically liberal advocacy group based in Washington, D.C.

SOURCE. People for the American Way, "Rise of the New McCarthyism: How Right Wing Extremists Try to Paralyze Government Through Ideological Smears and Baseless Attacks," December 2009. Reproduced by permission.

On December 2, 1954, the U.S. Senate voted to censure Sen. Joseph McCarthy, bringing to an end four years of political intimidation and character assassination so ferocious that McCarthy's name is still synonymous with a particularly destructive form of demagoguery.

The Rise and Fall of the McCarthy Campaign

McCarthy's campaign against supposedly widespread communist infiltration of the U.S. government brought down sitting Senators and intimidated even President [Dwight D.] Eisenhower . . . and his advisors. McCarthy's campaign was boosted by conservative think tanks, media figures, and clergy, and abetted for years by the unwillingness of most of his colleagues to stand up against his false charges and clear abuses of power.

> McCarthy's ideological heirs . . . are using [his] language and tactics . . . to stir fears that the nation is being destroyed by enemies from within.

McCarthy launched his campaign with a speech on February 9, 1950, in West Virginia, claiming to have a list of 205 people in the State Department known to be members of the Communist Party. He made similar claims, with shifting numbers, many times. McCarthy's charges were inflammatory and false, and often sufficiently vague to resist any fact-checking. But his bluster and manipulation of the era's fear of global communism allowed him to build power while destroying lives and careers.

McCarthy was eventually undone by his overreaching attacks on the U.S. Army; the televised Army-McCarthy hearings in 1954 finally exposed him to a wide audience as a malicious and irresponsible bully. A crucial moment in his reversal of fortune took place when the Army's chief counsel Joseph Welch, responding to attacks on a young lawyer, put McCarthy in his place, saying, "Have you no sense of decency, sir, at long last? Have you left no sense of decency?"

New Attacks, Same Old Responses

Today, Joseph McCarthy's ideological heirs in the Republican Party and right-wing media are using the language and tactics of McCarthy to stir fears that the nation is being destroyed by enemies from within. Republican Members of Congress and other GOP [Grand Old Party] officials have not shown Welch's concern for decency; instead they frequently act as an "amen chorus" to the far right's demagogues or stay silent, hoping to reap political gain from the attacks on President [Barack] Obama, administration officials and nominees, congressional democrats, and even military leaders.

Journalist Haynes Johnson, author of *The Age of Anxiety: McCarthyism to Terrorism*, writes:

> The shame of the Senate, especially the shame of its leaders and moderates on both sides of the aisle, was expressed by historian Robert Griffith when he wrote that McCarthy's victories were made possible "only by the unwillingness of moderates to take a stand that might expose them to obloquy." Perhaps, Griffith added, "this was the key to McCarthy's continued power—not the ranting of demagogues, but the fear and irresolution of honorable men."

Targeting the Democratic Party

Among McCarthy's targets was President Harry Truman, whom he called a "dangerous liberal," and the Democratic Party, of which he said during the 1952 campaign:

> The Democratic label is now the property of men who have been unwilling to recognize evil or who bent to whispered pleas from the lips of traitors. . . .

Right-wing political pundits such as Glenn Beck have been accused of resurrecting McCarthy's tactics to discredit political enemies. (Associated Press.)

In fact, McCarthy was fond of referring to the "Democrat Party"—using the term as a slur. The refusal to use the correct term "Democratic Party" was so associated with McCarthy that it went out of style for decades, but the rhetorical tactic has been resurrected and embraced by the Karl Rove-Newt Gingrich-Frank Luntz Republican Party of today.

McCarthy Tactics Then and Now

From 1953 to 1955, McCarthy held 117 hearings and even more closed-door interrogations, witch hunts for subversives that thrived on guilt by association: someone had worked for a union, dates a communist, been in a book club that read a book by [Karl] Marx. . . .

Today's McCarthyism has many faces and voices, including the household names of right-wing cable television, a plethora of radio hosts, Religious Right leaders, right-wing organizations and the bogus "grassroots" campaigns they generate—and Members of Congress and other Republican Party officials. Together they engage in character assassination and challenge the loyalty and patriotism of their targets.

> "Republican smear campaigns often make use of this 'elites vs. real Americans' theme."

Fox's Glenn Beck, who reaches millions of Americans with his televised tirades, has become an almost cartoonish McCarthy clone, with his guilt-by-association charts supposedly detailing the communist connections of White House officials.

Dangerous "Elites" Subverting the National Interest

McCarthy inflamed fears that the nation was being destroyed by enemies from within:

> The reason we find ourselves in a position of impotency is not because the enemy has sent men to invade our shores, but rather because of the traitorous actions of those who had all the benefits that the wealthiest nation on earth has had to offer—the finest homes, the finest college educations, and the finest jobs in Government (and the private sector) we can give.

Sound familiar? The attack on sinister Ivy League-educated elites is one of the essential rhetorical tools of far-right pundits and Republican politicians like Sarah Palin. . . .

Republican smear campaigns often make use of this "elites vs. real Americans" theme. Here's Curt Levey of the Committee for Justice, speaking to senators about then-Judge Sonia Sotomayor's nomination to the Supreme Court:

> Remember the values of the regular folks who sent you to Washington. Don't vote for a Supreme Court nominee whose values are closer to those of the intellectual elite than to those of your constituents.

McCarthy routinely accused his opponents of subverting the national interest. Typical was his characterization of Truman's Secretary of State Dean Acheson as someone "who steadfastly serves the interests of nations other than his own."

That's a staple of right-wing rhetoric today. . . .

> [McCarthy's] current-day acolytes have made charges long considered beyond the pale of political discourse.

Communism, Socialism, "Obamunism"

McCarthy frightened many Americans with charges that the government was infested with communist sympathizers. His current-day acolytes have made charges long considered beyond the pale of political discourse—comparisons of President Obama and other administration officials with tyrannical figures like [Nazi leader] Adolf Hitler, [Soviet dictator] Josef Stalin, and Chairman Mao [Tse-tung, Chinese Communist leader]—so frequently that they are losing their shock value. Former and likely future presidential candidate Mike Huckabee is among many who have called Obama a socialist, and said of the Obama budget, "Lenin and Stalin would love this stuff."

The same is true of charges that the Obama administration and congressional democratic leaders are

communists, socialists, and/or fascists bent on destroying capitalism and the market economy and imposing
a socialist dictatorship in America. Rep. Paul Broun of
Georgia has compared Obama to Hitler, called Obama
and Democratic congressional leaders a "socialistic elite"
and warned that they're planning to create a pretext to
declaring martial law. . . .

Van Jones, founder of Color of Change and a leading
advocate of using "green" technologies to bring jobs to
de-industrialized American cities, resigned from his position as a White House advisor after a fierce campaign
against him by right-wing pundits who denounced him
as a communist. Jones' resignation was like blood in the
water to Glenn Beck and others who have launched a series of smear campaigns against Obama administration
officials and nominees. . . .

Socialism: The Scheme to Destroy Churches and Families

Former Senator Rick Santorum has accused the Obama
administration and its allies of being so committed to
imposing socialism in America that they are scheming
to destroy churches and families: Santorum said that the
left's policies, especially those policies aggressively set
forward by the Obama administration, target the family
and Christian churches for "destruction," because these
institutions provide local social networks and support
for individuals that take away the need for total depen-
dence on central government. To eliminate these social
networks means the triumph of socialism, and that
means attacking marriage and Christian churches.

"There will be an assault on the institution of marriage," Santorum promised his audience. [He continued:]

> "Why? Because the left knows that they can't really have
> government come in and take control of everything
> unless they destroy the family. Unless you destroy the

family and destroy the Church they cannot ultimately be successful in getting socialism to be accepted in this country and that's what their objective is."

Guilt by Association

McCarthy was a master of guilt by association, smearing individuals as enemies of the country based on any association however indirect or tenuous, with a suspect organization, newspaper, or other publication, labor union, or individual. Criticism of McCarthy's tactics was itself evidence: his targets included not only communists, pro-communists, and former communists, but also "anti-anti-communists."

Today's McCarthyite right abounds with guilt-by-association attacks. In fact Glenn Beck has made a sort of art form out of them.

After right-wing activists engineered a public humiliation of the group ACORN [Association of Community Organizations for Reform Now], right-wing leaders have tried to use any relationship with the organization's decades of organizing on behalf of poor people as a disqualification for public service. Attacks on widely respected judicial nominee David Hamilton treated his one-month job as a canvasser for ACORN thirty years ago when he was 22 years old as if it had constituted a major portion of his career. . . .

An "Obsessive Hunt for Homosexuals"

McCarthy and his subcommittee's investigator Roy Cohn did not only target people for destruction based on alleged communist sympathies; they also hunted for homosexuals in government service. In a striking parallel, right-wing leaders, dismayed and outraged by growing public support for legal equality for LGBT [lesbian, gay, bisexual, transgender] Americans, have used public debates over marriage equality to attack gay people as enemies of faith, family, and freedom, and they are engaged in ongoing smear campaigns against openly gay Obama administration officials and nominees. . . .

Attacks on Military Leaders and Veterans

McCarthy attacked Gen. George Marshall, Truman's Secretary of Defense, for being engaged in a

great conspiracy, a conspiracy on a scale so immense as to dwarf any previous such venture in the history of man. A conspiracy of infamy so black that, when it is finally exposed, its principles shall be forever deserving of the maledictions of all honest men.

What is the objective of the great conspiracy? I think it is clear from what has occurred and is now occurring: to diminish the United States in world affairs, to weaken us militarily, to confuse our spirit with talk of surrender in the Far East and to impair our will to resist evil.

> 'Remember Benedict Arnold before giving credibility to a veteran who uses their service as a means to promote a leftist agenda.'

Earlier this year, journalist Greg Sargent, reviewing attacks by GOP leaders on Obama administration national security policies, such as the closing of the detention facility in Guantanamo [Cuba], that are supported by a number of former Republican national security officials and military officials, concluded:

It's a clear sign that Obama's national security positions (for good or for ill) are squarely in the mainstream of the D.C. Defense establishment. And it shows that the GOP's need to attack those positions has forced Republican officials outside that mainstream, isolating them further and putting them at odds with its onetime allies in that establishment.

Pennsylvania Rep. Daryl Metcalfe recently demonstrated that he has perfected the new McCarthyism by blasting veterans who disagree with his opposition to climate change legislation as traitors. [Metcalfe wrote in an e-mail to a veterans' organization:]

> As a veteran, I believe that any veteran lending their name, to promote the leftist propaganda of global warming and climate change, in an effort to control more of the wealth created in our economy, through cap and tax type policies, all in the name of national security, is a traitor to the oath he or she took to defend the Constitution of our great nation!
>
> Remember Benedict Arnold before giving credibility to a veteran who uses their service as a means to promote a leftist agenda.
>
> Drill Baby Drill!!!

Sowing the Seeds of Fear—Then and Now

Haynes Johnson reports that Harry Truman spoke against "lies and slander" by "scaremongers and hatemongers" in a 1951 speech:

> Character assassination is their stock in trade. Guilt by association is their motto. They have created such a wave of fear and uncertainty that their attacks upon our liberties go almost unchallenged. Many people are growing frightened—and frightened people panic.

It is clear that right-wing operatives, including the well-heeled forces behind "grassroots" uprisings against health care reform, are all about sowing fear—fear about the Obama administration, fear about his "socialist" agenda, fear about the supposed march from liberty to tyranny.

Even at the height of McCarthy's power, some of his Republican colleagues, people like Maine Sen. Margaret

Chase Smith, were willing to criticize his destructive campaign. Today, most GOP officials, when not actively participating in the fearmongering, are welcoming it as a means, they hope, of returning to power in 2010 and 2012. They are seemingly unconcerned about the destructive consequences of their fearmongering and the panic, potentially violent, it may encourage.

Not All Criticism Is McCarthyism

Jonathan Danzig

In the following college newspaper opinion piece, Jonathan Danzig claims that there are different shades of meaning to the term McCarthyism. It means more than just "anything I disagree with." McCarthyism, Danzig explains, started out in the 1950s as a simple political philosophy. Today the political definition of McCarthyism is "witch hunts," appeals to peoples' prejudices and emotions, wild accusations, and/or blacklisting. It is important, argues Danzig, to think carefully before labeling as McCarthyism or McCarthyite an action, statement, criticism, or opinion. Context matters, as does whether the statement is true or not. At the time this viewpoint was published, Jonathan Danzig was a sophomore at Tufts University in Massachusetts.

Photo on following page: Tea Party activists accuse President Barack Obama of socialist political sympathies. Defenders claim that this might be a scare tactic but not an example of McCarthyism. (AFP/ Getty Images.)

S enator Joseph McCarthy, the namesake of political McCarthyism, died in 1957. And yet a quick Google News search of "McCarthyism" returns hundreds of

SOURCE. Jonathan Danzig, "McCarthyism and Its Uses," *The Primary Source*, March 17, 2010. Reproduced by permission of the author.

recent articles comparing current events to McCarthyist intrigue:

> From [news anchor and political commentator] Keith Olbermann: the [US political movement] Tea Parties, or "Tea Klux Klan," accusing [US president Barack] Obama of socialism.

> From ACORN [Association of Community Organizations for Reform Now] CEO Bertha Lewis: Republicans calling for an investigation for her organization.

> From various sources: a Republican memo calling for the use of "fear" as a fundraising tactic.

And, of course, the list goes on. Were one to survey only Google News, "McCarthyite" would seem to be nothing more than an insult one hurls at political opponents, as if to say, "You are criticizing me, so you are therefore practicing repugnant McCarthyism!" And thus ends the debate, because McCarthyite tactics do not merit legitimate debate.

> McCarthyism in the 1950s was not a supernatural phenomenon; it was a straightforward political strategy.

Defining McCarthyism in the 1950s

If we accept that McCarthyism, in truth, has a more limited definition than "anything I disagree with," we must understand its origins. McCarthyism in the 1950s was not a supernatural phenomenon; it was a straightforward political strategy. Senator McCarthy of Minnesota, motivated by both anti-communism and a desire for a higher profile, arbitrarily accused hundreds of people in government of being communist or communist-influenced. He and his supporters pushed for loyalty tests in government, political blacklists in certain industries, and an FBI capable of harassing anyone with the slightest inclination of communist sympathies. In short, McCarthyites made stuff up and persecuted people for things they did not do, and thousands were affected.

But McCarthyism cannot be thought of as a singularly heinous plot stemming from a single person. Senator McCarthy saw a real threat—communist influence in U.S. federal agencies—and exploited it for political gain. He was only right insofar that there actually were, as it turned out, paid Soviet agents in the State Department, but neither to the extent he claimed nor to the people he randomly accused. The pivotal moment of McCarthyism came in 1954, when McCarthy baselessly implied that Joseph N. Welch, head counsel for the U.S. Army, had hired a communist in his law firm. "Have you left no sense of decency?" asked Welch. McCarthy did anything—anything—to advance his political goals.

Defining McCarthyism Today

The modern political definition of McCarthyism can be stated most simply as witch hunts, demagoguery, wild accusations, and/or blacklisting. If a politician is making facts up just to destroy a political opponent, that is undeniably McCarthyism. But if someone just states an unpopular or controversial opinion, that cannot simply be pigeonholed as McCarthyism. For that matter, it is certainly not McCarthyism to say things that are true.

Is it McCarthyism for Republicans to use "fear" as a fundraising tactic, or for Tea Partiers to say that President Obama is leading America towards socialism? The two go hand-in-hand, used towards the political end of electing like-minded politi-

> Is it McCarthyism for Republicans to use 'fear' as a fundraising tactic, or for Tea Partiers to say that President Obama is leading America towards socialism?

cians. But if you think about it, to call the use of fear in political advertisements "McCarthyist" amounts to calling all negative advertising "McCarthyist"; after all, their point is to make voters so concerned—scared, even—of what the one candidate would do in office that they have no choice but to vote for the other as the lesser of two evils.

A Matter of Interpretation

When, however, such ads play on "fear" of "socialism," then the advertisements' creators are walking a fine line. Throwing around the label "socialist" makes for little constructive discussion, given its Soviet implications and echo of McCarthy himself. But in today's politics, "socialism" accusations refer not to Soviet espionage, but rather to the obvious: President Obama's policies are intended to bring the United States closer to the model set by the social democracies of Europe and further from the vision of, say, [US president] Ronald Reagan. It may not be constructive, but, given the right context, it is not McCarthyism to call Obama a socialist. In all fairness, though, it is completely McCarthyist to say Obama was not born in the United States, or that he was brainwashed while he lived in Indonesia.

So it goes with the other examples. It is not McCarthyism for [attorney and daughter of the vice president, Dick Cheney] Liz Cheney to call certain public defenders the "al-Qaeda Seven" unless she falsely claims that they actually work for al-Qaeda. It is not McCarthyism for Republicans to demand an investigation into ACORN, so long as the charges against them have some proof. In any case, analysts would take great care to consider the implications of the word "McCarthyism" and its own McCarthyist implications.

CHAPTER 3

Personal Narratives

A Scientist and His Wife Speak Out About Being Falsely Accused

Jerry Manheim and Sylvia Manheim, interviewed by Griffin Farfiello

In the following viewpoint, former physicist Jerry Manheim shares what it was like to be falsely accused of being the head of a Communist ring within the company for which he had worked for ten months. He explains how he was told he was a security risk, hastily escorted out of the building without being given any information, and ultimately fired. He relates what happened to what had been a promising career as a result. He and his wife, Sylvia, go on to describe what happened at the hearings at which they had to testify and tell how agents of the Federal Bureau of Investigation harassed them and questioned their neighbors. Jerry Manheim talks about the efforts made over time to finally clear his name and to regain his security clearance. Jerry Manheim is a professor of mathematics. Sylvia Manheim is a school teacher.

Photo on previous page: Jackie Robinson of the Brooklyn Dodgers testified before the House Un-American Activities Committee in 1949, declaring that African Americans would fight "against Russia or any other enemy." (Associated Press.)

SOURCE. Jerry and Sylvia Manheim, interview by Griffin Farfiello, *Red Scare: Memories of the American Inquisition: An Oral History.* NY: W.W. Norton & Company, 1995. Reproduced by permission.

Jerry: I was brought up in Chicago in a very middle-class home. I had no information about anything left of the Democratic Party until college. I think I was a sophomore when I saw a sign for a Socialist Study Club meeting. I didn't know what that meant, so I went, and was very impressed with the philosophical position the group was espousing. I joined. I was drafted probably within a year of that meeting. I met [my wife] Sylvia at a dance for servicemen at Local 65, and started seeing her regularly. She was working at the time as a switchboard operator at the Communist Party headquarters in New York. She arranged for me and a friend of mine to have a meeting with V. J. Jerome, who was the chief theoretician of the Communist Party at that time. . . .

So my friend and I went up and had this meeting with him at Communist Party headquarters. It was verbally violent. My friend was afraid they were going to throw us out the window. After we left, they told Sylvia if she wanted to keep her job, she should stop seeing me. . . .

An Unfounded Accusation

When the war ended, I attended the University of Illinois. Sylvia also went there, and we continued going to the Socialist Study Club. In 1946 we were married. Around 1949, I got a job in research and development with IT&T in New Jersey. I was working on what they called the "strip line," which was the precursor of the printed circuit. We were also doing work on a system for a missile.

I had been there approximately ten months when I was called into the security office. They came and got me out of my lab. When I got to the office, they informed me that I was a security risk. They wouldn't give me any information, except that I had to be out of there immediately.

> I couldn't even go by myself because I was [believed to be] such a terrible risk.

A woman reads the *Sunday Worker* at the American Communist Party headquarters in New York City. **(Time & Life Pictures.)**

A security man followed me back to my office while I cleared out my radio and lunch bucket. I couldn't even go by myself because I was [believed to be] such a terrible risk. . . .

The very first thing I did was to call up the ACLU [American Civil Liberties Union]. I was a member. I told them what happened. . . . They said, "We can't help you at all." I was dumbfounded. So I said to the ACLU person, "Well, what are the names of the organizations on the Attorney General's list?"—figuring I might've belonged to one of them. They said, "We won't tell you that." They wouldn't even give me a list of the organizations.

I went to see this attorney, Murray Gordon. . . . He said he would take my case.

We found out that IT&T claimed that I was head of a Communist ring there. That was the main accusation and that's why they fired me. Years later, through my FBI [Federal Bureau of Iinvestigation] files, I discovered that I was also supposed to be the head of the Communist Party in Hartford, Connecticut. I had been to Hartford exactly once for two hours to go to the veteran's hospital for a test.

Enduring a Hearing

Because IT&T was involved with the Department of Defense, the hearing was held at the Pentagon. We collected people who would go down and testify on my behalf. Of course, asking someone to testify presents a risk of sorts for them, some of it real and some imagined. People responded in ways which I never would have predicted. There were those who said, "I don't want to have any more conversations with you, just don't call me anymore." Some of my close friends responded that way. Others, like a young person I knew, a member of the Young People's Socialist League and in a defense industry, had no qualms about coming. . . .

The hearing was held before a board of military people. The chairman was a civilian, as I recall, and the rest were all big brass from the Army, Navy, Marine Corps, and Air Force. They were mainly colonel rank, or the equivalent, and they had been tapped and told, "Your next three-month assignment is to sit in Washington and listen to security cases." They had no training in this at all. Some of them had very minimal education.

> They said, 'That's real Communist stuff.'

They brought up the fact that when I was in the Army, I was a member of the orientation team for our company. They said, "As a member of the orientation team, you said such-and-such about the Russians."

I said, "That's true, I did."

They said, "That's real Communist stuff."

[I replied:] "I didn't have any option. We were given all the material by the Army. My job was to pass it on to the troops at the orientation meeting."

They said, "That's a lie. The Army would never say that about the Russians."

"Well, can I have some time to find the pamphlet and send you a copy of it?" They agreed to give me two weeks.

They also said that I was a member of the Party, that I was in charge of the ring at IT&T, and that they had evidence for this. None of it was true. They pointed to the fact that I had a book in my house called *Political Economy* by an economist named Leontiev. That was right. I picked it up for a quarter at a used-book sale. I thought it would be interesting, but I never had read it. Sylvia also testified at the hearing.

More Questions and a Verdict

Sylvia: I was very nervous. Colonel Rounds, who was sitting in the back, a rather rotund colonel with red cheeks, got up and said, "Mrs. Manheim, what organizations does your son Carl belong to?"

I said, "My son is five years old. He belongs to the Cub Scouts. That's a crazy question."

He said, "Well, I have to tell you, Mrs. Manheim, that Communist parents indoctrinate their children at young ages." At that point, I knew in my soul that we didn't have a chance. With that kind of reasoning, I knew it was over.

They asked me what newspapers I read. I told them that I read the *New York Post*, which was a good newspaper in those days, and that I occasionally read the *New York Times*. They said, "Why don't you read the *Journal American*?" which was just one of these scandal sheets. They also asked, "Do you frequent a movie house called the Little Carnegie?" They said they saw me attend a Russian movie there. I said, "Well, yes, I like foreign films." They also noticed that I belonged to a drama reading group, that we had a black friend, that people of other colors came to visit us. All these things fit together on a profile of a really subversive couple.

> I felt like a pariah, like I was lurking around society as a shadow.

Jerry: Of course, they brought up the fact that Sylvia had worked as a switchboard operator at the Communist Party headquarters, which in their eyes was tantamount to being in the hierarchy.

That was the end of the hearing, and then I had two weeks to find the pamphlet. I went to Columbia University and found the pamphlet in the library. I wasn't allowed to take it, as it was classified. But I cut out the pages I needed. It was that important to me. The same day that I sent in this evidence showing that what I had said was accurate, I got the verdict. They had no interest in it. The decision from the security board was that I was a security risk. . . .

Bad Times

When we got the verdict, I was thrown out on my ear. I had a friend, an engineer, who was selling televisions out of his house and putting up antennas. He hired me for something like fifty dollars a week. It was an obscenely low salary. . . . I worked with him for quite a while. . . . Then I worked with another fellow who was trying to start an engineering company. I worked in his basement, soldering and doing various other things. After that, I got a job with a company that did some defense work. They wanted to know what my clearance level was. So I had to say, "I don't want to do any defense work," and I quit. This happened a couple of times. Everyone was doing defense work, so I was only around for a few months at a time. I felt like a pariah, like I was lurking around society as a shadow. It was terrible.

During this time, the FBI was always around. Sometimes they'd get into our car and talk to us, which was better than getting in their bugged car to talk to them. They were always asking about other people, and I never told them anything. . . .

Sylvia: They even went to our neighbors and asked if we borrowed anything and if we didn't return it. Remember the time they came to my house and asked about my mother? These two lovely young FBI men—they all came in pairs wearing three-piece suits, gray with a little vest—knocked on my door. I invited them in. They said to me, "We know that you worked for the Communist Party, and if you don't give us the names of the people that you worked with, your mother could be deported. We know she became a citizen illegally." They gave me twenty-four hours to make up my mind. I didn't sleep all night. They came back the next morning, the same handsome men in their three-piece suits, and I invited them in, offered them coffee. All I said to them was, "I have to look in the mirror in the morning and face myself. I can't give you names." . . .

A New Hearing: Clearance Restored

Jerry: I was just going from job to job, feeling awful. Finally, I got a job teaching at Cooper Union. I worked in the math department in the engineering school. It was now '55, and the climate had changed. We knew that if we got some new documentary evidence, we could reopen the case. Sylvia found some of the letters I'd written her when I was overseas in the Army, telling her my opinion of the Communist Party. I had an attorney friend who told me, "I think you ought to try to get Joseph Rauh to handle your case."

I'd received a telegram . . . to appear at Foley Square to testify, so I went to Rauh and his partners to discuss the situation. When they asked what I was planning on doing, I said, "I'm going to take the Fifth Amendment."

Rauh said, "Why are you going to do that?"

"Because it's nobody's business what my politics are."

Rauh responded, "That's really nifty. Don't you know they want people like you, Fifth Amendment Communists? How many Communists do you know?"

> 'Don't you know they want people like you, Fifth Amendment Communists?'

I said, "I don't know anybody that I can say for sure is a Communist."

"And you're going to take the Fifth?"

They really leaned on me, saying that this was a stupid thing to do, and that it was very selfish of me. I understood their argument, but I wasn't ready for it. That weekend, Rauh went to Washington. He was having lunch in some restaurant when Joe McCarthy came over and said, "Oh boy, we're going to have your man Manheim on the stand, a Commie, and we're going to run him into the ground." . . .

Rauh said, "He's going to be wonderful. Manheim's not taking the Fifth."

"What do you mean, he's not taking the Fifth?"

"That's exactly what I'm telling you. He's not taking the Fifth."

McCarthy was absolutely flabbergasted. The next day I got a telegram canceling my appearance at Foley Square. Rauh was absolutely right, all they wanted were Fifth Amendment Communists. . . .

So Rauh collected data and we decided to have another hearing. This time it was in New York, in some federal office. These were civilians. They said, "We want to tape-record this conversation. Just to make sure there are no errors. You'll have an opportunity to read the transcript to make any corrections you want." They asked about being a member of the Party. I told them I was not, nor had I ever been, a Communist. I'd never been pro-Communist.

This time, my clearance was restored. . . .

Getting my clearance was very important to me psychologically, but it didn't matter in terms of employment. I didn't have the stomach for going back into industry. I never did.

An Environmentalist Recalls the McCarthy Period

Hazel Wolf

In the following viewpoint, Hazel Wolf shares with a group of high school students her memories of how such diverse groups of American society as churches, unions, teachers, the Democratic Party, and the arts were affected by the McCarthy "witch hunt" for Communists. She explains why she became a member of the Communist Party in the 1930s and describes some of the activities in which she took part, including an attempt to hold off an eviction, occupation of a city hall for days as part of a demonstration, and organizing a senior citizens union. She gives her reasons for deciding to leave the party and goes on to describe her arrest for deportation years later, charged with having belonged to the party and supposedly conspiring to overthrow the US government. Hazel Wolf was the cofounder of the Seattle, Washington, Audubon Society and a dedicated and tireless advocate for environmental causes.

SOURCE. Hazel Wolf, "The McCarthy Period," May 24, 1990. www.members.tripod.com/HazelWolf/Hazel_Witchhunt.html. Reproduced by permission.

I understand you have been studying the McCarthy period, which has also been described as a witch hunt. I looked "witch hunt" up in the Webster's college dictionary where it is in part defined like this: "An investigation usually conducted with much publicity, supposedly to uncover subversive political activity, disloyalty, etc., but really to harass and weaken the entire political opposition."

I think that is a fair description of the McCarthy witch hunt. . . .

McCarthy was a senator from Wisconsin who was obsessed by the anti-Communist virus and carried on a hysterical campaign, supported by the newspapers, TV and radio for several tragic years, until finally his arrogance and extremism led to public refusal to take any more of it, and he went down to defeat. But not until damage was done to the lives of uncounted thousands of people.

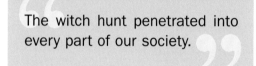

The witch hunt penetrated into every part of our society.

Groups Affected by McCarthy's Witch Hunt

The witch hunt penetrated into every part of our society. For example, the churches were ordered to have their governing members take loyalty oaths, stating they were not Communists. Most churches caved in, even though it was, and still is, the law that churches pay no taxes.

The church brought legal action against this injustice. After several years in court they won their case and the Internal Revenue Service was forced to return the taxes. That settled the matter for all other churches.

Unions were forced to take loyalty oaths that none of their officers was a Communist. Many, if not most, gave in to this pressure and actually expelled officers or members who had fought against corruption, racism or other discriminatory acts within the union. Seamen had to take loyalty oaths or their right to employment was forfeited. Thousands lost their jobs.

The Democratic political party suffered the loss of many good leaders through the witch hunt within the party.

All teachers were forced to take the oath or lose their jobs. Many were accused of having unpopular political opinions and found themselves unemployed and blacklisted. Hundreds of the best and most courageous teachers were lost to the schools, and, of course, to the students. . . .

The arts came under attack. . . .

Ronald Reagan, who was then a B-rated movie actor and president of the Screen Actors Guild, led a movement to blacklist actors and technicians. The blacklist threw hundreds of them out of jobs with no hope of finding others in the movie industry.

A famous court trial of what was known as the Hollywood Ten sentenced them to prison for refusal to take the oath or state whether or not they were or ever had been Communists. Among them were some of the finest artists. . . .

Stool Pigeons and Persecution

A whole crew of professional stool pigeons erupted, who for a fee would appear in court or at governmental state and national Unamerican Activities Committee hearings, and swear that this, that and other accused was a Communist. It is interesting that the fee for men who testified was $50, while the women and Filipinos received $25. I always felt they should have joined a "Stoolpigeons" union and fight for better pay and no discrimination.

The known Communists came under special persecution. Even the lawyers who defended them were harassed and threatened with disbarment. Judges who were brave enough to rule according to law, if the law favored the accused, were threatened. Juries were intimidated into handing down guilty verdicts or face the loss of jobs or pensions should they decide otherwise in view of the evidence.

> I joined the Party in about 1934, in the middle of the Great Depression.

There were Communists arrested all over the nation, five of them in Seattle [Washington]. They were accused of plotting to overthrow the government by force and violence, but not one charge was ever proved against them, not one.

The trials were largely on what books they read and what was in the books. Many served prison sentences, but most, after a long court battle, were freed. . . .

Being a Communist

I thought you might want to know what a Communist did from day to day. I joined the Party in about 1934, in the middle of the Great Depression. . . . Millions of families were unemployed. Teachers, engineers, actors, nurses, bookkeepers, secretaries, construction workers, carpenters, waiters, cooks and truck drivers—people in every walk of life and of all races. The depression bit deep. I, a single mother with a small daughter, was one of them. I was a secretary. At the beginning there was no welfare, no unemployment insurance, no social security for the retired worker, no industrial insurance for injured workers.

I, too, was dependent on an inadequate food voucher, which was all the help that was available. I came across a person one day at the food voucher station, who asked me to sign a petition to the state legislature. It petitioned the legislature to provide unemployment insurance to jobless workers. I had never heard of such a thing and neither had anybody else as far as I knew. I asked who drew up the petition (which I signed, of course) and was told it was drawn up by the Communist Party. That really interested me so I went to one of their meetings held in a home only to find out that the family was being evicted for non-payment of rent. So I joined in what was occurring. As the Sheriff's men brought the furniture out to pile it on the sidewalk, the rest of us picked it up and took it into the house by the back door. This went on for quite a while until the sheriff and his men, who were not very enthusiastic in the first place, left in despair and frustration. We went inside for the meeting. I learned that the Communists were planning to organize the people at the voucher station to better things in general. From then on I was very busy. So busy, in fact, that I forgot my own very real problems. I no longer felt alone and helpless; matter of fact, it was even a sort of fun time.

A Period of Change

We demonstrated down at Olympia [Washington], occupied the city hall for days, wrote letters to politicians and wherever needed. We struggled for food, for housing, for clothing, against racism and for the rights of women. We also helped organize a Senior Citizens Union which launched a petition to set up pensions on a state level for the elderly. This prompted the Postmaster General to say, "The United States is made up of 49 states and the Soviet of Washington." This was the very first state pension ever paid in the United States, and remained in force until the national Society Security payments began to take the place of state pensions. Incidentally this pension union was placed on what was known as the Attorney General's Subversive Activities list, in an effort to destroy the union.

As the Depression began to thin out due to the hiring of people in government work programs, and later through preparation for World War II, the activities of the Communist Party became less necessary and I lost interest and gradually stopped going to meetings and paying dues. About 1942 I was no longer a member, although I never lost my respect for the work we did when I was, and I have many friends who still belong today.

Arrest and Jail

Early in 1958, some thirteen years after I left the Communist Party, I was arrested for deportation and charged with conspiring to overthrow the government by force and violence and with belonging to the Communist Party thirteen years previously.

I was not a citizen, having been born in Victoria, in Canada. I might say that the foreign born were the earliest victims of the McCarthy witch hunt. The reason for this is that those who are foreign born do not have the protection that native born citizens have of the laws of the Constitution, so they are easier to prosecute. We had a number of foreign born, or aliens, in this country then. This arrest of foreign born had a great affect on all the non-citizens and hampered them in any effort they might make to join a union to better their lives. . . .

Some 400 aliens who were Communists or suspected Communists were arrested throughout the country. Most of them were rescued by the courts.

When I was arrested I was put in a room with two other prisoners. The first thing they wanted to know was why I was in jail. I told them I had been accused of conspiring to overthrow the government. One of the young women said: "What a wonderful idea. The government ought to be overthrown. They had a jigsaw puzzle in the room which I started to work on because I hardly ever had a chance to finish one and here was my big chance. But it was not to be. My friends bailed me out before the day was over. So much for my being in the slammer.

> 'I know I won't be deported. The American people won't let that happen.'

The Threat of Deportation

My arrest caused a little flurry in the newspapers and reporters interviewed me. The first question was, "What did I intend to do if I were deported?" I remember saying the first thing that crossed my mind: "I know I won't be deported, the American people won't let that happen." I could not have been more right. A committee was formed by volunteers, most of whom I had never heard of, calling themselves The Washington Committee for the Protection of the Foreign Born. Eventually we had some 14 cases in this state. . . .

At one stage in my case Canada refused to accept me because I was no longer a citizen of that country due to the fact I had married an American. In those days when women married foreigners in either Canada or the United States, they lost their citizenship, while at the same time they did not take on the citizenship of their husbands. They were women without a country. This law has since been changed.

This decision from Canada was a low blow to the Immigration Service. Then, after licking their wounds a while, they attempted to deport me to England on the basis that my father was a British citizen, therefore I derived that citizenship from him.

As the case went from court to court, even to the Supreme Court of the United States, we lost each court battle, but in the end we won the war, because the McCarthy hysteria had died down through public pressure and even the Immigration Department decided that I wasn't going to overthrow the government after all, and they dismissed the case, after nearly twenty years. In 1970 I became a [US] citizen.

A Scholar Remembers Going One-on-One with McCarthy

William Mandel

In the following viewpoint, William Mandel tells what happened as a result of being subpoenaed by Senator McCarthy, who was investigating the State Department's Overseas Libraries, which included a book by Mandel. He explains how powerful McCarthy was at the time. Mandel confides that he was determined to do everything he could to discredit McCarthy during the hearing while ensuring he did not have to name others or go to jail. He discusses the tactics he used to take down McCarthy and shares the fear he felt when he was successful. Mandel shares reactions to his testimony by the media, different individuals, and his employer. He goes on to relate how the entire episode affected his children. William Mandel is an author, broadcast journalist, political activist, and an internationally recognized Soviet affairs analyst.

SOURCE. William Mandel, "Season of the Witch Hunts: One on One with Joe McCarthy," *Counterpunch*, May 10, 2003. Reproduced by permission.

In 1953 the countryside seen from a train window between Washington and New York was still chiefly pastoral. But in March the bare branches of the trees, the dark brown of the fields, the black of the asphalt roads, and the cold gray of the sky, deepened by early nightfall, corresponded to the mood of the nation: gloomy and fearful.

Acknowledging the Power of Joe McCarthy

I felt the same way. I should have been elated. I had gone to Washington in response to a subpoena from Sen. Joe McCarthy and had been determined to do as much as any single person could to destroy him. Now, convinced that I had damaged the senator severely, I was scared. I was sure he knew that he had lost, and badly. This was borne out by a personal attack on me in his newspaper column five weeks later.

> I had had no doubt before being called, and even less after confronting [McCarthy] personally on consecutive days, that his was truly a fascist mentality.

I had had no doubt before being called, and even less after confronting him personally on consecutive days, that his was truly a fascist mentality. And fascists use physical violence to dispose of their opponents. He was immensely powerful, having brought the State Department to its knees and having already attacked the former head of the country's armed forces, Gen. [George] Marshall. Prime Minister Clement Atlee of England said to Parliament that year that he sometimes wondered whether it was Gen. [Dwight] Eisenhower or Joe McCarthy who was president of the United States.

Back in New York that evening, I learned that the most sensational parts of my attack on him had been carried on national TV news, in addition to the complete live coverage during the day. Later, NBC pre-empted its very popular radio show, "Music At Midnight," to re-broadcast forty-five minutes of my testimony. The next day words of mine were front-page news in the *New York Times*, which wrote: "Mr. McCarthy reddened at times." *Time* magazine wrote: "The week's most agitated performance came from a blazing-eyed New York advertising copywriter." It is a mark of the times that *Time* chose to identify me not as a scholar subpoenaed because a book of his was in the State Department's Overseas Libraries, the target of McCarthy's investigation, but by the work to which I had to turn for a livelihood after I was blacklisted.

Reactions to the Attack on McCarthy

I went into work the day after the hearing, and my employer at a Madison Avenue advertising agency told me to stay home for a few weeks, and that my salary would continue. When I got home, a telegram had arrived from a fellow employee with whom I had never had any association except at work. It read: "Dear Bill. The following is my telephone number Plaza 35198. The following is my address 153 East 51st St. If I can be of any service to you please call. Anna Santoro."

I began receiving letters from total strangers who had gotten my address from media reports as well as from acquaintances. Most reflected enthusiasm that someone had finally taken McCarthy down. A few were antagonistic. One, signed by a woman with a Ukrainian name in Chicago, was sent to me care of the McCarthy Committee, which dutifully forwarded it. It contained a very interesting sentence: "You can see there is a temptation to get violent with your type of people." It was not a stupid letter, and had some very pertinent things to say about lack of civil liberties in the Soviet Union, the country my sinful book had dealt with.

A man in Richmond, Indiana, hoped I wouldn't lose my job, and wanted to write my employer. I provided the

firm's address. He did write and send me a carbon copy. In a large, bold, sweeping, almost 19th-century hand, he made a particularly fine statement about the nature of the fight against McCarthyism. He wrote that I had defended my: "basic American privilege of writing books and putting into them what he feels is the objective truth, as he sees it. To me this attitude (freedom to think and speak), plus the bravery and courage to defend it, constitutes the true American way of life . . . that the authors of our Constitution and Bill of Rights envisioned." The man also hoped that my "way of making a living would not suffer."

Senator Joseph McCarthy during a hearing on May 3, 1954. (Associated Press.)

A lot of good it did me. My employer canvassed all his clients—Parke-Davis, then the major drug manufacturer, Parkside Laboratories, Heublein, which was nonmusical—and asked whether I should be fired. None supported doing that, but neither did they urge my retention. They wanted no problems with McCarthy. Who knows what he might investigate next? After my month's paid leave, I was fired and paid another month's salary as severance pay, although I had been there only a year. Conscience money.

> My main satisfaction lies in what I know I did for people in what Lillian Hellman dubbed 'the scoundrel time.'

My main satisfaction lies in what I know I did for people in what Lillian Hellman dubbed "the scoundrel time." From Shreveport, Louisiana, a Jack Hooper wrote me: "Any time that I become depressed, due to the operations of the Nazi Fascist McCarthy Committee, I play your record and truly get a 'lift.'" I had made an LP [long-playing record] from an excellent wire recording a friend had made from the NBC rebroadcast. Ordinary citizens did not yet possess tape recorders.

Weighing Alternatives in Response to a Subpoena

Those who heard the proceedings or read the news stories had no way of knowing what went on in my heart and mind in preparing for it. When I was handed the subpoena by a process server who rang my doorbell at about noon on a Saturday, I was packing an overnight bag in preparation for a lecture that evening at a synagogue in New Haven [Connecticut]. I had been invited to speak by the rabbi who married [actress] Marilyn Monroe and [playwright] Arthur Miller. The subpoena demanded that I appear on Monday at 2 P.M. How was I to find a lawyer in Washington from New York City on a Saturday afternoon? I was lucky. I had a lawyer uncle who knew the right man in Washington.

I weighed the alternatives: should I go to New Haven to carry out my speaking engagement? The purpose of such subpoenas was to silence the people to whom they were served. I went to New Haven, spoke, came home, and spent Sunday making notes. With a wife and three young children, six, eight, and thirteen, I wanted to avoid a contempt citation and jail sentence. Every additional person who went to jail added to the atmosphere of fear of McCarthy himself and McCarthyism practices. So did everyone who stayed out of jail by caving in. I wanted to discredit McCarthy and yet avoid imprisonment.

Playing the Game to Discredit McCarthy

I knew that the hearing would be televised. I was perfectly aware and, from his behavior, so was he, that this was theater. My job was to be the dignified scholar, which I was, and prosecutor when I got a chance. The senator knew that people were very dubious about his methods, and wanted to look and sound judicial.

> My job was to be the dignified scholar, which I was, and prosecutor when I got a chance.

I feared that my lawyer's office would be bugged, because he had represented many "unfriendly witnesses," as we were called. Therefore I wrote out my questions in clear longhand and handed them to him instead of stating them out loud. I asked whether I could query McCarthy about the relative size of his savings and salary, which I did in the public hearing, to good effect. My list of possible challenges to him continued: Why did you defend Nazis who murdered U.S. prisoners of war? Why do you want war with China?

I could not refuse to answer a question if it flowed logically from my own answer to a previous question. This would be a chess game. I had to avoid checkmate—

being put in a position where I would have to name other individuals or go to jail for refusing to do so.

I was called as one of the witnesses on the first day of an investigation into how books by bad people like me and [historian and author] Dr. W.E.B. DuBois, who was subpoenaed to appear on the same day, found their way into U.S. Embassy Information Office libraries overseas. DuBois' attorney, former Congressman Vito Marcantonio, who had cast the sole vote against the Korean War, called McCarthy's chief counsel, Roy Cohn, beforehand and asked: "Do you really want the whole Negro population down on the neck of the committee?" DuBois' subpoena was withdrawn.

My barely teenage daughter and her boyfriend of the same age had their own personal FBI [Federal Bureau of Investigation] tail, presumably on the assumption that they might lead them to the boy's father, whom the Communist Party had sent underground when it was made illegal by the McCarran and Smith acts and trials of its national and state leaders. This terror had serious effects upon [my daughter] Phyllis and Keith, her husband-to-be, all their lives.

Prior to my McCarthy hearing, a telephone caller identified himself as an FBI agent and asked me to come down to see them. I said no. They made further attempts to see me, at home. The fright it caused in our children was expressed in irrational fears for years to come, requiring a period of hospitalization for one of them.

A Teen Supports Ethel and Julius Rosenberg's Innocence

Dorothy M. Zellner

In the following viewpoint, Dorothy M. Zeller recalls her emotions and involvement as a fifteen-year-old working in support of Julius and Ethel Rosenberg, an American couple sentenced to death for espionage. She tells how important the Rosenbergs and their case were to her and her political friends and how she fervently worked on their behalf writing letters, signing clemency petitions, attending rallies, handing out leaflets, and asking passersby to sign petitions. She describes participating in a Washington, D.C., demonstration, hoping to get a last-minute reprieve for the Rosenbergs and how sad she felt after all efforts to save the Rosenbergs from electrocution proved futile. Dorothy M. Zellner is an activist. At the time this viewpoint was written, she was director of publications at the Center for Constitutional Rights, a nonprofit legal advocacy organization based in New York City.

SOURCE. Dorothy M. Zellner, "Proletaria and Me: A Memoir in Progress," *Red Diapers: Growing Up in the Communist Left*. Judy Kaplan & Linn Shapiro (eds). Chicago: University of Illinois Press, 1998. Reproduced by permission.

By 1953, when I was fifteen and in my second year of high school, Ethel and Julius Rosenberg had been on Death Row in Sing Sing for two years. I lived and breathed their case. I wrote letters, signed clemency petitions, went to rallies, and stood on street corners winter and summer with the Rosenberg committee giving out leaflets and asking for signatures from passersby. I knew as much about the Rosenbergs—people I had never seen—as I did about my own relatives and certainly cared more for them than for some of the people in my life.

My political friends shared this passionate involvement: even as young teenagers we were able to cite all the arguments—legal, moral, and political— supporting the Rosenbergs' innocence, and we understood all the legal maneuvers and the appeals. Hour after hour we read the letters the Rosenbergs wrote to each other and studied the photos that appeared in the newspapers and the Rosenberg committee literature. In a sense, the Rosenbergs were our movie stars and we their teenage fans. But it was more than that: in the extreme anticommunist hysteria of the '50s, the Rosenbergs represented the possibility that we could actually be charged with something fantastic that we never did and "fry in the electric chair," as the New York dailies so delicately put it. Simultaneously we also became [the Rosenbergs' sons] Michael and Robby, children whose parents could be taken away forever.

> In the extreme anticommunist hysteria of the '50s, the Rosenbergs represented the possibility that we could actually be [falsely] charged with something fantastic . . . and 'fry in the electric chair.'

Demonstrating for Clemency

The date for the Rosenbergs' electrocution was set for June 18, 1953. As a last desperate effort, the leaders of the Rosenberg defense committee organized demonstrations throughout the country to pressure congressional representatives and President [Dwight D.] Eisenhower for clemency. [Family friend] Alice [Jerome], my mother, Freddy [Jerome], and I joined a special train of thousands of people in Penn Station that morning, hoping that an eleventh-hour miracle might occur. After arriving in Washington, we spent a few futile hours pursuing hostile congressmen up and down the halls of the House Office Building and then joined a picket line at the Treasury Building of several thousand people marching ten or fifteen abreast, carrying signs urging presidential clemency. In the afternoon, the picket captains passed the word that Supreme Court Justice [William O.] Douglas had granted a one-day stay of execution. Alice and my mother had to get back to New York, but Alice told Freddy that he could stay if he wanted to. I begged my mother to be allowed to stay. Somehow or other, Alice convinced her: "Sara, it's so important!"

> Our picket captain . . . said over and over tearfully, 'The Supreme Court has not upheld the stay.'

Freddy and I volunteered for the 2 to 4 A.M. shift in front of the White House, where about a hundred hardy souls walked around and around close to the black iron White House fence. The area was dark, silent, and almost completely deserted of pedestrians or automobiles, except for the occasional car that cruised by, plastered with signs suggesting that the Rosenbergs burn in hell.

After sleeping a few hours on the floor in a youth hostel, chosen because it was one of the few interracial places to stay overnight in Washington in 1953, we went back to the White House. By day there were several hundred people picketing, and we marched up and down, holding our signs up, waiting for some word about whether the full Supreme Court had continued Justice Douglas's stay

Many supported clemency for Ethel and Julius Rosenberg, who had been sentenced to death for espionage, including Julius Rosenberg's mother (center). (**New York Daily News via Getty Images.**)

of execution. Finally, the word came. Our picket captain, a plump woman in her forties, stood inside the line and said over and over tearfully, "The Supreme Court has not upheld the stay. The vote was six to three. The execution is scheduled for eight o'clock tonight." Disconsolately we tramped back and forth, back and forth for the next two hours.

Mourning an Execution

Across Pennsylvania Avenue, in Lafayette Park, a tremendous crowd gathered, smelling blood. They booed and screamed at us. At the precise moment of eight o'clock we picketers turned, put our picket signs down, and silently faced the White House. The crowd across the street shrieked with joy.

Numb, we were escorted by police to our waiting chartered bus and arrived back at home about 3 A.M. The next day the New York papers dwelt lovingly on every detail of the executions, including the fact that wisps of smoke came out of Ethel's head after the switch was pulled. I broke down and sobbed for hours, kneeling on the floor with my head on my bed. My mother, alarmed at my grief, refused to let me go to the Rosenbergs' funeral. Some days later, I bought myself a bracelet of silver links in honor of Julius and Ethel and swore the adolescent promise that I would wear it "always."

I did—for a few weeks.

When school started in the fall, I wrote a paper for my English class about the trip to Washington to save the Rosenbergs. Normally I was somewhat cautious when it came to revealing my full political views, even in a school as liberal as the High School of Music and Art, but the experience overcame my reticence. When the teacher, a nervous, rabbit-faced person, returned everyone's work, he cleared his throat and announced that contrary to his usual procedure, he wanted one of us to read the assignment aloud to the class. Much to my surprise, he meant me, and I went up to the front of the room and read the whole article. When I finished, the other students were utterly silent, but after class a few of them came up to me and asked me sympathetic questions.

Only much later did I realize that my teacher's request revealed more about him than I could appreciate at the time.

A Writer Recounts Growing Up With Left-Wing Parents

Patricia Lynden

In the following viewpoint, Patricia Lynden describes life in the 1950s for children whose parents or other family members were Communists or Communist sympathizers. She describes her first and most traumatic experience of being an outsider: her uncle having to go underground in order to avoid being arrested for being a Communist leader. She expresses her overwhelming fear that her father might lose his job and details some of the social consequences of growing up in the environment she and others like her did. She goes on to tell why she will never forget the day her father was subpoenaed to testify before the House Un-American Activities Committee and how her classmates and others reacted to the news of his unfriendly testimony. Patricia Lynden is a writer and editor.

SOURCE. Patricia Lynden, "A Survivor Remembers: America's Most Recent Major 'Witch Hunt,'" *On the Issues Magazine*, Summer 1992. Reproduced by permission.

My generation was born in the 1930s and '40s to parents who either stayed in the [Communist] Party after World War II when it was no longer safe to do so, or who left the Party before the cold war began but remained sympathetic to communism's version of a just society. Jokingly called "red-diaper babies" by our parents, we grew up outside the American mainstream. That was partly through our own choice —we had been raised to reject much that capitalism had wrought—but in large measure it was because, during the scary and depressing post-war decade of the Blacklists, doors were closed to us and our parents.

> When they were young, my parents, and virtually all of my aunts and uncles, were either Communist Party members or 'fellow travelers.'

In the 1930s and early '40s, when they were young, my parents, and virtually all of my aunts and uncles, were either Communist Party members or "fellow travelers"—to borrow a favorite phrase of Joe McCarthy. But by 1950, all except my late uncle Archie Brown, a fiery, dedicated life-long Communist, and one aunt, had left the party. . . .

A Communist Uncle "Disappears"

One of the most central and sobering lessons of my youth occurred in the early 1950s and was the result of my uncle Archie's Communist Party membership. It was my first and most dramatic experience of being an outsider. One afternoon, when I was about 13 and the McCarthy era was at full tilt, I was called into our living room by my father. Archie was about to "disappear," he told me; in fact, he was probably gone already. "What do you mean 'disappear'?" I asked. "The Party has chosen some leaders to stand trial and go to jail, and others to stay free. But they have to go underground so they won't be arrested," was my father's reply. "Where's he going?"

"There's an old revolutionary principle," my father said quietly, "that you should never know more than you have to about what your fellow revolutionaries are doing. If they arrest you and torture you, you can't betray anyone because you can't tell what you don't know. It's better that way I don't want to know either." Few conversations have impressed me more.

That night, as my father predicted, the FBI showed up. There were two agents, in fedoras no less, sitting in a pale blue car parked in front of the house. "They'll be tapping the phone," said my father, "so don't use it to discuss anyone in the family, and be careful of neighbors who ask too many questions because the FBI [Federal Bureau of Investigation] has probably found stooges among them." Even at the rebellious age of 13, I knew enough to listen well and do as he said.

Such conversations were universal among parents and children of the left in those days. We all recall the gratuitous harassment, so frightening to a child, of strange, unfriendly men in dark suits ringing the bell and asking to speak to our parents, tailing family members, sometimes even us, bugging our phones and making spies of our neighbors. One of my friends remembers an awful night when the FBI shone a powerful beam of light through the windows of her house, and with it scoured every piece of furniture, the floors, and walls of every room that wasn't curtained. "Even the ceilings," she later said indignantly. "Maybe they thought we had the atom bomb secret hidden in the chandelier?"

> The biggest fear . . . was whether your father would lose his job.

Dealing with Fear of Job Loss and the FBI

The biggest fear, though, was whether your father would lose his job. My father, Richard Lynden, was an elected official of the International Longshoremen's and Warehousemen's Union, the small, independent, politically radical union founded, and for many years led, by Harry Bridges. His job was safe, but that was not enough to make us feel secure—even if we put up a pretty good front.

The night the FBI came to camp in front of our house, my father grandly announced that he was taking us all to dinner at Amelio's, then one of San Francisco's finest restaurants. He took a long, out-of-the-way route there while my sister and I, in our finery, made faces and stuck our tongues out at the two agents in the car that never got more than 20 feet behind us. Playfully, my father drove as though he were being elaborately courteous to two nitwits, very, very slowly to the outskirts of the Mission district and then up a lonely dirt road. At the crest of the hill, which was flat and just big enough for two cars, he drove around and around and around in a circle. You couldn't tell who was following whom, and my father played the game for 10 minutes, chuckling as he occasionally slammed on his brakes, forcing the agents to do the same to keep from rear-ending us. Finally, he took us to dinner. The blue car stayed with us for a month, and left.

For those kids whose parents did lose their jobs, the feelings of persecution and terror were a constant in their lives for years. "Dangerous," is how my friend "Marcus," now a tenured professor, sums up his view of the world. "I still have a very strong sense of it." . . .

Social Consequences: A Fact of Life

The social consequences were tough for some of us, catastrophic for others. My father, who had been radicalized while he was an undergraduate at Stanford in the early '30s, helped organize the workers in his father's wholesale grocery business. My grandfather was a bedrock conservative who disagreed violently with my father's politics, although he never disowned him, as some other parents did. But I was always acutely aware of the tension between them, which sometimes erupted into furious fights that made my grandfather cry and caused my father to go on weeks-long drunks.

I will never forget the day my father's subpoena to appear before HUAC [House Un-American Activities Committee] was delivered. It was brought by a middle-aged woman carrying a shopping bag. She looked like one of those ladies who often came around in those days to collect money for one cause or another. . . .

> I will never forget the day my father's subpoena to appear before HUAC was delivered.

"Hello, dear, is your daddy home?" she inquired sweetly. I said I'd call him. When he came to the door, she reached into her bag, threw the subpoena at him and, with bitchy saccharinity said, "I'm sorry it had to be this way, Mr. Lynden." I was miserable. I felt as though I had betrayed my father and my guilt lasted for weeks.

We children were not left without means to protect ourselves in socially troublesome situations. Our parents taught us a political perspective, some theory and history to back it up, and we were secure that ours was the right view of the world. With that we were armed with feelings of both intellectual and moral superiority. When my father's appearance before the HUAC came, I was well prepared with my knowledge of the history of the Fifth Amendment.

At school, after my father's unfriendly testimony made the front pages of the local newspapers, there were just a few unpleasant remarks from schoolmates. Only Miss Quinn, until then my favorite teacher, said, "Aren't you embarrassed?" I was humiliated and enraged. My best friend was forbidden to come to my house anymore, but she lied and came anyway. Although these memories are fresh today, I know they are nothing compared to what other kids went through. . . .

A Lesson Learned All Too Well

One law that all of us left-wing kids lived by, and that I have lived by until now, is that you never, never discuss who is a Communist and who is not.

Consequently, it has been with considerable anxiety and guilt that I have written here that my uncle Archie, even though he died in 1990, and one aunt, never left the Communist party. Growing up, we were all taught that belief in Communism and Party membership is a Constitutionally protected right; that our system isn't worth anything if it only protects people with safe views.

During the McCarthy years, anyone who "named names" was to us that lowest form of humanity, a fink. I still believe that. But right up to his death, Archie was a proud and outspoken Communist, and my aunt was too, though she was never a public figure. If Archie didn't mind talking about it, why should I? So why have all these feelings come rushing back, and why doesn't my nausea about writing this go away?

GLOSSARY

Alien Registration Act of 1940 — The Smith Act; a statute that made it an offense to support or belong to a group advocating the violent overthrow of the US government.

***Amerasia* spy case** — 1945 case that centered on classified government documents found in the New York office of a pro-Communist journal.

CIA — Central Intelligence Agency of the US government; collects information on foreign governments, corporations, and individuals, and advises senior government policy makers on matters of national security.

Cold War — Attempt after World War II by the United States and the Soviet Union to gain world influence by means short of a full-scale war.

Coplon case — Case of a Justice Department employee, Judy Coplon, convicted of espionage in 1950 for passing classified files to a Soviet agent.

FBI — Federal Bureau of Investigation; agency of the US Department of Justice that investigates federal crimes and provides criminal justice assistance to federal, state, municipal, and international agencies.

Fellow traveler — Individual who supports or sympathizes with the aims of Communists.

Fifth Amendment — Amendment to the US Constitution that includes a self-incrimination clause that gives individuals the right to refuse to reveal information that could be used against them in a criminal prosecution.

Fifth Amendment Communist	Person called as a witness by an investigative body such as the HUAC who pleaded the Fifth Amendment to avoid prison and/or testifying about his/her beliefs or acquaintances. The label was meant to suggest conspiratorial activity.
Gold Case	1950 case of a convicted chemist, Harry Gold, who traveled all over the United States collecting atomic secrets to pass to the Soviet Union.
Grand Old Party	Nickname for the Republican Party.
Hatch Act	Officially known as An Act to Prevent Pernicious Political Activities; 1939 federal law that prohibited federal employees from taking an active part in political campaigns, from using their official positions to pressure voters, and from membership in a political organization advocating the overthrow of the US constitutional form of government.
Hollywood blacklist	List of professionals not allowed to work in the American entertainment industry because they were suspected of being Communists or of having Communist sympathies.
Hiss case	Case of a State Department employee, Alger Hiss, accused of being a Soviet spy and convicted in 1950 of perjury.
House Un-American Activities Committee (HUAC)	Congressional investigative committee that conducted investigations into alleged Communist activities throughout the 1940s and 1950s.
KGB	Soviet state security organization, the Committee for State Security.
Loyalty Board	Boards set up within departments or agencies to hear loyalty cases and recommend whether an employee suspected or accused of disloyalty should be removed from office or fired.
Loyalty Review Board	Board created in 1947 by President Harry Truman that made sympathy with any "subversive" organization on its list grounds for dismissal from government employment.

Manhattan Project US government project to develop a nuclear bomb; it ran from 1942 to 1946.

Marshall Plan European Recovery Plan enacted in 1947 by the United States to help rebuild Europe after World War II.

McCarthyism Public allegation of disloyalty to one's country, especially through pro-Communist activity, often without proof or based on slight, doubtful, or irrelevant evidence; term created in 1950 by cartoonist Herb Block referring to the actions and activities of Joe McCarthy.

Red Scare Two separate periods of strong anti-communism sentiment bordering on hysteria in the United States, the first from 1917 to 1920 and the second from the late 1940s through the mid-1950s.

Venona documents Decrypted secret Soviet intelligence cables made public in 1995.

CHRONOLOGY

1940 The Smith Act (Alien Registration Act) is signed into law June 28.

1945 Harry S. Truman becomes president of the United States.

1946 Joseph McCarthy is elected to the US Senate.

The House Un-American Activities Committee (HUAC) is made a permanent House committee charged with investigating Communist subversion.

1947 FBI director J. Edgar Hoover helps the HUAC's efforts to publicize Communist influence in Hollywood.

President Truman issues Executive Order 9835, which creates a loyalty program for government employees.

Ten movie screenwriters and directors—known as the Hollywood Ten—appear before the HUAC and are cited for failing to testify about their Communist associations.

1948 The Hollywood Ten are convicted of contempt of Congress, blacklisted, and sent to prison.

1949 President Truman announces that the Soviet Union has tested an atomic bomb.

Chinese leader Mao Tse-tung formally declares China a Communist republic.

Alger Hiss and Whittaker Chambers testify before the HUAC.

1950   Alger Hiss is convicted of perjury and sentenced to five years in prison.

Joseph McCarthy makes his "Enemies from Within" speech in Wheeling, West Virginia.

The Tydings Committee is created and begins hearings to investigate McCarthy's charge that there are Communists in the State Department.

Washington Post editorial cartoonist Herb Block coins the term "McCarthyism."

Senator Margaret Chase Smith denounces McCarthy in her "Declaration of Conscience" speech to the Senate.

Red Channels: The Report of Communist Influence in Radio and Television is published and starts the blacklist of entertainers.

Americans Julius and Ethel Rosenberg are arrested for stealing atomic bomb secrets for the Soviets.

The Korean War begins.

The Tydings Committee denounces McCarthy.

Congress passes the Internal Security Act (McCarran Act), requiring registration of Communist organizations with the attorney general's office.

1951   The Rosenbergs are convicted of espionage and sentenced to death.

1952   Dwight Eisenhower is elected president of the United States.

McCarthy is reelected to the Senate.

1953   McCarthy is appointed chairman of the Senate Committee of Government Operations and begins an investigation into espionage at the Army Signal Corps Radar Lab at Fort Monmouth, New Jersey.

The Rosenbergs are executed.

1954   McCarthy is given a seat on the Senate Rules Committee.

Edward R. Murrow does a two-part report on McCarthy on the CBS news program *See It Now*.

The Army-McCarthy Hearings are televised.

The Senate censures McCarthy for behavior "contrary to senatorial traditions."

1995   The US National Security Agency releases the Venona documents.

FOR FURTHER READING

Books

Edward Alwood, *Dark Days in the Newsroom: McCarthyism Aimed at the Press*. Philadelphia, PA: Temple University Press, 2007.

William F. Buckley, Jr. and L. Brent Bozell, *McCarthy and His Enemies: The Record and Its Meaning*. Washington, DC: Regnery Publishing, Inc., 1995.

Daniel Cohen, *Joseph McCarthy: The Misuse of Political Power*. Brookfield, CT: Millbrook Press, 1996.

M. Stanton Evans, *Blacklisted by History: The Untold Story of Senator Joe McCarthy and His Fight Against America's Enemies*. New York: Crown Forum, 2007.

Richard M. Freeland, *The Truman Doctrine and the Origins of McCarthyism: Foreign Policy, Domestic Politics, and Internal Security, 1946–1948*. New York: Alfred Knopf, 1972.

Albert Fried (ed), *McCarthyism: The Great American Red Scare: A Documentary History*. New York: Oxford University Press, 1997.

Richard M. Fried, *Nightmare in Red: The McCarthy Era in Perspective*. New York: Oxford University Press, 1990.

Marjorie Garber and Rebecca L. Walkowitz (eds), *Secret Agents: The Rosenberg Case, McCarthyism and Fifties America*. New York: Routledge, 1995.

John E. Haynes, *Red Scare or Red Menace?* Chicago, IL: Ivan R. Dee, 1996.

Arthur Herman, *Joseph McCarthy: Reexamining the Life and Legacy of America's Most Hated Senator*. New York: The Free Press, 2000.

Haynes Johnson, *The Age of Anxiety: McCarthyism to Terrorism*. New York: Harcourt, Inc., 2005.

Harvey Klehr and Ronald Rodash, *The Amerasia Spy Case: Prelude to McCarthyism*. Chapel Hill, NC: University of North Carolina Press, 1996.

Robert and Michael Meeropol, *We Are Your Sons: The Legacy of Ethel and Julius Rosenberg*. Boston, MA: Houghton Mifflin Company, 1975.

Ted Morgan, *Reds: McCarthyism in Twentieth-Century America*. New York: Random House, 2003.

Thomas C. Reeves, *The Life and Times of Joe McCarthy: A Biography*. New York: Stein and Day, 1982.

Ronald Rodash and Joyce Milton, *The Rosenberg File* (Second Edition). New Haven, CT: Yale University Press, 1997.

Richard H. Rovere, *Senator Joe McCarthy*. Berkeley and Los Angeles, CA: University of California Press, 1996.

Walter Schneir, *Final Verdict: What Really Happened in the Rosenberg Case*. Hoboken, NJ: Melville House Publishing, 2010.

Ellen Schrecker, *Many Are the Crimes: McCarthyism in America*. Boston: Little, Brown, 1998.

——— *The Age of McCarthyism: A Brief History with Documents*. New York: Bedford/St. Martin's, 2001.

Robert Shogan, *No Sense of Decency: The Army-McCarthy Hearings: A Demagogue Falls and Television Takes Charge of American Politics*. Lanham, MD: Ivan R. Dee, 2009.

Francis H. Thompson, *The Frustration of Politics: Truman, Congress, and the Loyalty Issue, 1945–1953*. Cranbury, NJ: Associated University Presses, 1979.

Periodicals

Joseph Berger, "Decades Later, Rosenberg Case Again Ignites Passions," *New York Times*, November 15, 2004.

Gail Russell Chaddock, "The Red Scare revisited: inside McCarthy files," *Christian Science Monitor*, May 6, 2003.

E.J. Dionne, Jr., "As Variously Invoked, 'McCarthyism' Seems to Have Lost Specific Meaning," *Washington Post*, October 24, 1991.

M. Stanton Evans, "McCarthyism: Waging the Cold War in America," *Human Events*, May 30, 1997.

Ed Goodpaster, "A brief encounter with Senator McCarthy," *Kilgore News Herald*, March 3, 2006.

Ron Grossman, "The Witch Hunter From Wisconsin: It Has Been 50 Years Since Joe McCarthy Had Dinner With The GOP Ladies and Served Up His First Communist Plot Du Jour," *Chicago Tribune*, February 8, 2000.

Bob Hoover, "'Atom spy' verdict is in, and again it's guilty," *Pittsburgh Post-Gazette*, September 15, 2008.

W.H. Lawrence, "Impact of the Army-McCarthy Hearings: An Appraisal," *New York Times*, June 13, 1954.

"National Affairs: Part of the Picture," *Time*, May 10, 1954.

Drew Pearson, "All White House Attempts to Appease McCarthy Fail," *St. Petersburg Times*, March 9, 1954.

"The Presidency: McCarthyism v. Trumanism," *Time*, August 27, 1951.

Kit Rachlis, "The Rise and Fall of Joseph McCarthy," *Los Angeles Times*, November 7, 1999.

"Revisionist McCarthyism," *New York Times*, October 23, 1998.

Sam Roberts, "A decade of fear: how 'McCarthyism' turned American against American in the decade after World War II," *New York Times Upfront*, March 15, 2010.

Williard Shelton, "Lattimore Case: McCarthy's Vicious Retreat," *Nation*, April 23, 2009.

Websites

The Man Behind McCarthyism: A Gateway (www.albany. edu/history/HIS530/mccarthyism/index.html). This site provides a wealth of information about McCarthy and McCarthyism through links to numerous sites categorized under the headings Background, Timeline, Books, Documents & Newspaper Articles, Multimedia, and Legacy of McCarthyism. It also offers a blogger spot for input relevant to the topic.

Spartacus Educational: McCarthyism (www.spartacus. schoolnet.co.uk/USAred.htm). This site provides an extensive index of links to topics related to McCarthyism, each of which contains a topic-based narrative, illustrations, and primary sources, all with hyperlinked text. Some also include video.

United States Senate (www.senate.gov/artandhistory/ history/common/generic/McCarthy_Transcripts.htm). This site provides access to five volumes of transcripts of the 1953–1954 McCarthy Hearings, all downloadable in PDF format.

INDEX

Y

Z